RESTORATION
COLLECTION

D1327134

RESTORATION
COLLECTION

HYMN DRAMATIZATIONS

...BY...

NELLIE E. MARSH

AND

W. A. POOVEY

CENTRAL FLORIDA BIBLE COLLEGE LIBRARY

THE STANDARD PUBLISHING COMPANY

CINCINNATI, OHIO, U. S. A.

Copyright, 1942

The Standard Publishing Company

Printed in U. S. A.

Introduction

Stories of how the great hymns of the church came to be written are always inspiring. This is because most hymns are written out of some deep spiritual experience of the authors.

Desiring to make some of these hymn stories live, the authors of this book, residing in widely separate sections of the United States, conceived the idea of dramatizing them. They introduced their dramas as special features of their respective Sunday evening church services with splendid results. Simultaneously, they submitted their manuscripts for publication, hoping that the thing which had worked for them might be of value to the churches of America.

The settings, situations and lines are simple enough for amateur performers, yet dramatize the hymn stories in a most effective manner. They will give new meaning to the old hymns and inspire a deeper interest in hymnody.

—THE PUBLISHERS.

Contents

HYMN DRAMATIZATIONS

Blest Be the Tie

Blest be the tie that binds
  Our hearts in Christian love;
The fellowship of kindred minds
  Is like to that above.

Before our Father's throne
  We pour our ardent prayers;
Our fears, our hopes, our aims are one,
  Our comforts and our cares.

We share our mutual woes,
  Our mutual burdens bear;
And often for each other flows
  The sympathizing tear.

When we asunder part,
  It gives us inward pain;
But we shall still be joined in heart,
  And hope to meet again.

This glorious hope revives
  Our courage by the way;
While each in expectation lives,
  And longs to see the day.

From sorrow, toil and pain
  And sin, we shall be free;
And perfect love and friendship reign
  Thro' all eternity.—*John Fawcett.*

Blest Be the Tie

CHARACTERS

JOHN FAWCETT _____ A minister
MRS. MARY FAWCETT _____ His wife
MRS. WINGATE ⎫
MRS. MINOR ⎪
MRS. ALDEN ⎬ Members of Mr.
MRS. SMITH ⎪ Fawcett's church.
MRS. LEWIS ⎭

(The women may be accompanied by children.)

COSTUMES AND SUGGESTIONS

In keeping with the late eighteenth century. Scene II, Mr. and Mrs. Fawcett have the appearance of being older than in the first scene.

SCENE I

[*Living-room of the Fawcett home. Appearance of room indicative of moving day.* MR. *and* MRS. FAWCETT *are packing books in boxes.*]

MR. FAWCETT—Nancy, I keep wondering if we are making a wise move by accepting a call to the London church.

MRS. FAWCETT—I wondered that at first but decided it was only sentiment that made me feel that way. Oh, I'm so tired! Let's rest a while. We have plenty of time to finish what little we have to do.

[*Both sit down.*]

9

Mr. Fawcett—Call it sentiment if you like, but I have a feeling we shall not be happy.

Mrs. Fawcett—Why, John, how can you think that? We have filled our mission here, and, besides, I thought you wanted a larger church.

Mr. Fawcett—So I did—so I did. [*Walks to window and looks out.*]

Mrs. Fawcett—Really, sometimes I wonder if you know what you want.

[Mr. Fawcett *walks back to chair and sits down. His facial expression is one of sadness.*]

Mr. Fawcett—Maybe I don't. I know one thing; if I had known I was going to dread leaving these people as I do, I should never have planned for the move.

Mrs. Fawcett—But, John, we must think of our children. We can never educate them on the salary here; in fact, we are barely existing now.

Mr. Fawcett—Yes, I know that and I know I haven't as much time left to preach as most ministers who have preached the same number of years I have. I was older than most ministers when I was ordained.

Mrs. Fawcett [*laughing*]—You are always regretting that you did not begin preaching two or three years before you did. What difference could those few years make?

Mr. Fawcett—Many souls might have been saved in that time.

Mrs. Fawcett—You are too conscientious, that's all. That is the reason you dread leaving here. These people are sad because you are leaving, and now you feel you are doing wrong.

Mr. Fawcett—Not doing wrong, maybe, but I can't help feeling that if the Lord meant for us to leave, I should not be so sad.

Mrs. Fawcett—Well, anyway, it is too late now to change our minds, and I'm glad of it.

Mr. Fawcett [*slowly*]—Yes, I suppose so. I've resigned here and accepted the London church. The salary here is less than two hundred dollars a year, and we can't live on that and the people can't pay more. They sacrifice even to pay that.

Mrs. Fawcett—Yes, I know they do, but maybe they can get some one whose obligations are not so great as yours. I love them, too, but we can't live on love, you know.

Mr. Fawcett—I know that, but neither can we live without the ties of love.

Mrs. Fawcett—We can love people wherever we are, can't we? There will always be love ties.

Mr. Fawcett—This parting seems different some way— I don't know what it is. I have never been able to plan our future in the big church. It is just—well, like we shall never be there.

Mrs. Fawcett—That is absurd. You know we shall be there.

Mr. Fawcett—No funeral sermon was ever as hard to preach as that farewell sermon yesterday. Then, as the different ones came today to bid us farewell, each good-by was harder to say.

Mrs. Fawcett—You should be happy that they love you so much. For hours they have been coming, each with an expression of gratitude for your help and kindness.

Mr. Fawcett—I'm not worthy of it all.

Mrs. Fawcett—Yes, you are. Your efforts have been untiring. No minister in a large church ever put in more hours than you have.

[*A knock is heard at the door.* Mrs. Fawcett *goes to the door, and* Mrs. Wingate *and* Mrs. Minor *enter.*]

11

Mrs. Wingate—I hope we are not intruding. I know you are busy, but we wanted to come for a few minutes.

[Mr. Fawcett *rises and shakes hands with them.*]

Mrs. Fawcett—No, you are not intruding. We are happy to have you. Come, sit down.

Mrs. Minor—It just doesn't seem possible that you are going away. I can't imagine Wainsgate Church without you.

Mr. Fawcett—That is very kind of you, but we really haven't been here so many years.

Mrs. Wingate—True enough, but it seems we have known and loved you for years. You have been such a source of comfort and help during the times of sadness in our homes. Others feel the same way. We have depended on you for so much.

Mrs. Minor—How many times I have heard that expressed since we learned you were leaving! Mr. Fawcett, isn't there any way we can keep you?

Mr. Fawcett—I'd love to stay, but my family is growing larger and I feel I must go. You dear people here are doing all you can, and no one can do more. It is hard—I don't want to go.

Mrs. Wingate—We are selfish to ask you, I know, but sometimes the heart rules the head, I guess.

Mrs. Minor [*rises*]—We must be going, for you folks are busy, I know. We shall never forget you. The ties of Christian love can never be broken by distance.

[Mr. Fawcett *looks off into the distance for a moment as if a thought has come to him very forcefully.* Mrs. Fawcett *and* Mrs. Wingate *rise, and* Mrs. Wingate *and* Mrs. Minor *walk toward the door, followed by* Mr. *and* Mrs. Fawcett.]

Mrs. Wingate [*shaking hands with* Mr. *and* Mrs. Fawcett]—Well, good-by and may God bless you.

[MRS. MINOR *bids the* FAWCETTS *farewell and the two women leave.* MR. *and* MRS. FAWCETT *walk slowly back to their chairs.* MR. FAWCETT *takes an envelope from his pocket, begins writing on it, then places it in his pocket again.*]

MRS. FAWCETT—Such dear people—all of them. You are right; their coming makes parting all the harder.

[*A knock is heard.* MRS. FAWCETT *goes to door, opens it and* MRS. ALDEN *enters.*]

MRS. ALDEN—I just had to stop for a few minutes for a last good-by.

MRS. FAWCETT—So glad you did. Won't you come and sit down?

[MR. FAWCETT *walks toward* MRS. ALDEN *and shakes hands.*]

MRS. ALDEN—I don't want to interfere with your packing.

MR. FAWCETT—We are nearly finished—and we always have time for our friends.

MRS. ALDEN—I haven't time to sit down. I must be hurrying along home. Mr. and Mrs. Fawcett, I want to express my thanks for all your kindness. May the Lord richly bless you in your new field; you deserve it. I shall never forget your many helpful messages nor your kindness at all times.

MR. FAWCETT—Thank you, Mrs. Alden, we have done only our duty and, if we have been helpful, we are happy.

MRS. ALDEN—Good-by and don't forget us. [*Leaves rather hurriedly.* MRS. SMITH *and* MRS. LEWIS *enter as* MRS. ALDEN *is leaving.*]

MRS. SMITH [*laughing*]—More company.

MRS. FAWCETT—We are always glad to have company.

MRS. LEWIS—Well, we wanted to see you before you left. You are leaving today, aren't you?

MRS. FAWCETT [*offering chairs to the women*]—Yes, the men are over at the church now, loading the furniture from Mr. Fawcett's study.

MRS. SMITH—We won't have time to sit down, thank you. If there were only some way to keep you! Accept my thanks for all you have done for my family, and may God bless you both.

MRS. LEWIS—Accept my appreciation for having been true Christian friends at all times.

[*Both women shake hands with* MR. *and* MRS. FAWCETT.]

• MR. FAWCETT—I shall repeat what I have told the others —that the ties of Christian love can never be broken. Good-by.

[MRS. LEWIS *and* MRS. SMITH *leave.* MR. *and* MRS. FAWCETT *walk slowly to the center of room.* MRS. FAWCETT *sits down and begins to weep.* MR. FAWCETT *walks to her and places his hand on her shoulder.*]

MR. FAWCETT—What is it, my dear?

MRS. FAWCETT—John, I can't bear this. I've tried to be brave for your sake. I don't know how I can leave.

MR. FAWCETT—Neither do I. [*Walks to window or door and looks out; walks slowly back to table and picks up a book, opens it, turns several of the pages, places it back on the table. Goes over to* MRS. FAWCETT, *who has been watching him intently. He speaks with determination.*] We will remain here.

MRS. FAWCETT—Do you mean it?

MR. FAWCETT—Never was more sincere in my life. We shall trust to God that things will work out for us. Just tell the moving men, when they come, to take the things back to my study. We are *not* moving.

[*Sits down, takes envelope from his pocket and begins to write.* MRS. FAWCETT *begins unpacking books. These actions should not be too fast.*]

MRS. FAWCETT [*looking toward* MR. FAWCETT]—What are you doing?

MR. FAWCETT—Oh, nothing much. Just jotting down a few thoughts that came to me.

MRS. FAWCETT [*looking over his shoulder, reads*]:
    "Blest be the tie that binds
        Our hearts in Christian love;
    The fellowship of kindred minds
        Is like to that above."

MRS. FAWCETT—Why, that is beautiful; how did you happen to write it?

MR. FAWCETT—Well, several of the ladies mentioned the ties of Christian love, and the words kept running through my mind.

MRS. FAWCETT—That would make a beautiful song. Can't you write several verses and set it to music?

MR. FAWCETT—Now, now, my dear, I'm no poet, but I shall write at least two more.

CURTAIN

SCENE II

[*Living-room of the Fawcett home, forty years later.* MRS. FAWCETT *is sewing.* MR. FAWCETT *enters.*]

MR. FAWCETT—Busy as usual.

MRS. FAWCETT [*smiles*]—That is when I am happiest, especially when sewing for my grandchildren.

MR. FAWCETT [*sits down and picks up paper or magazine*]—A proud grandmother you are [*laughingly*]!

15

MRS. FAWCETT—And why shouldn't I be? [*Both laugh.*] Have you been busy today?

MR. FAWCETT—Yes, I'm always busy. There are several sick; then there was a committee meeting at the church and several other matters of business I had to attend to.

MRS. FAWCETT—I had three guests this afternoon.

MR. FAWCETT—You did—who?

MRS. FAWCETT—Mrs. Alden, Mrs. Wingate and Mrs. Minor. Do you remember forty years ago today they called?

MR. FAWCETT [*thinks a moment*]—Oh, yes, how could I forget? We were getting ready to move from Wainsgate, and they came to bid us good-by.

MRS. FAWCETT—That's right, and we—two sentimental creatures that we are—decided to stay at Wainsgate.

MR. FAWCETT—Ever regretted it?

MRS. FAWCETT—Indeed not. So much has happened since then. Our children are all grown up, we have grandchildren; and the church, while not large, is so much larger. One can hardly believe it possible.

MR. FAWCETT—Yes, we have seen the older members taken by death and the younger ones assuming the responsibility. Times in general have changed.

MRS. FAWCETT—Well, there is one thing that hasn't changed. You are still the same humble person you were then—always kind and helpful.

MR. FAWCETT—Nancy, I've always felt that we should not be so happy today if we had accepted that call to London.

MRS. FAWCETT—I don't think we should either. It was never meant for us to leave here.

MR. FAWCETT—Remember how we thought we had to have a larger church in order to meet expenses? We were sure there was no other way.

Mrs. Fawcett—Yes, I remember, and it didn't seem that there was. I doubt if at that time you had ever thought you could serve your fellow men in any other way but by preaching.

Mr. Fawcett—I'm afraid I don't follow your line of thought.

Mrs. Fawcett—Well, the first writing you ever attempted was inspired by the church members who came to bid us farewell. You heard several of them refer to the ties of Christian love, and you wrote a poem about it. That event was the beginning. Your influence now reaches many more than it would even if you were preaching for a large church. Thousands are now singing the song.

Mr. Fawcett—I see what you mean now, but I wish I could do more.

Mrs. Fawcett—The same ambitious John I married many years ago! Have you ever thought how many things have happened all because, through our sadness when we were leaving Wainsgate, you put your thoughts into poetry?

Mr. Fawcett—Can't say that I've ever given it much thought.

Mrs. Fawcett [*speaking rather slowly and distinctly*]— Well, in the writing of that poem you discovered you had literary ability. You have since written many poems, books and essays. Your essay on "Anger" so interested King George that he offered to grant any wish you might make. Our friend's son who was sentenced to death for forgery was saved because that was the wish you made. He is now a worth-while citizen. Your income from your writings has made it possible for us to live comfortably and still remain in the little church here where we are so happy.

Mr. Fawcett [*smiling*]—Quite a philosopher, aren't you? I'll confess I had never thought of it, but no doubt

17

that little poem was the turning point in our lives—and it was such a small thing. However, it probably would never have been heard of if Dr. Mason hadn't wanted words for a tune he brought from Switzerland.

MRS. FAWCETT—Don't be so modest. There is a letter for you there on the table; I almost forgot to tell you.

MR. FAWCETT [*picks up letter and looks at it*]—It's from Brown University in Rhode Island. [*Opens letter and reads it.*]

MRS. FAWCETT—What is it? Good or bad news?

MR. FAWCETT [*smiles*]—You be the judge; it says that Brown University desires to confer upon me the honorary degree of Doctor of Divinity, in June.

MRS. FAWCETT—Oh, John, I'm so happy for you. Thanks again for the song which caused you to discover yourself. Listen. [*"Blest Be the Tie" is heard being sung quietly offstage.*] It's our children singing your song. [*The singers offstage begin singing the song more loudly. All six stanzas may be sung.*]

CURTAIN

18

The Church in the Wildwood

There's a church in the valley by the wildwood,
  No lovelier spot in the dale;
No place is so dear to my childhood
  As the little brown church in the vale.

Chorus

O come to the church by the wildwood,
  O come to the church in the dale;
No spot is so dear to my childhood
  As the little brown church in the vale.

O come to the church in the wildwood,
  To the trees where the wild flowers bloom;
Where the parting hymn will be chanted,
  We will weep by the side of the tomb.

How sweet on a clear Sabbath morning
  To list to the clear ringing bell;
Its tones so sweetly are calling,
  O come to the church in the vale.

From the church in the valley by the wildwood,
  When day fades away into night,
I would fain from this spot of my childhood
  Wing my way to the mansions of light.

                 —*William S. Pitts.*

The Church in the Wildwood

CHARACTERS

Reader
Judson Grant _____A hard-boiled business man
Mr. Hildebrand _____A young and energetic minister
Miss Johnson _____An efficient secretary
Mr. Wilson _____An aged minister

COSTUMES

Modern.

MUSICAL BACKGROUND

The singing should be done by a group of boys or young men. If this can not be managed, use a mixed group. The singers are backstage.

SCENE I

[*An office, furnished with desk and chairs.*]

READER—In the hearts of most Christians there is treasured a memory of a little church where they spent their youth. Even though they may attend magnificent cathedrals in later life, the impression of that tiny church of long ago remains very dear. William S. Pitts has put that feeling into his famous hymn, "The Church in the Wildwood." This hymn touches tender memories and has become a great favorite in America. Perhaps if more could hear it and remember their churchgoing days of long ago, our churches would be filled every Sunday. But let us tell you the story of one man who heard this hymn—Judson Grant, a hard-boiled business man.

[*Curtain rises, revealing* GRANT *at desk and* HILDEBRAND *in chair.*]

GRANT—Well, Mr. Hildebrand, you've succeeded in getting past my secretary. Now what do you want?

HILDEBRAND—Only to take a look at you, Mr. Grant.

GRANT—I'm sorry, but I have no time for joking.

HILDEBRAND—I wasn't joking. I simply wanted to see what a practical business man looked like—a man who is so practical that he takes care of his business and loses his own soul.

GRANT—I take it that you've come here to ask me for money for your church.

HILDEBRAND—No, it's not your money I'm after, Judson Grant. It's your soul.

GRANT—What makes you worry so much about my soul?

HILDEBRAND—Only this: When you came to this town as a young man, you came from a godly family. You were interested in the church and you put your trust in Jesus Christ. Now you've grown cold and hard. The only thing that you trust is your bank balance.

GRANT—You ministers are all too impractical. I've got a business to run. I've got stockholders to think about and workmen to pay. I haven't time for church.

HILDEBRAND—Mr. Grant, you know that a dollar is worth more than a penny. When are you going to learn that a human soul is more precious than all the stocks and bonds in the world? "What shall it profit a man if he gain the whole world and lose his own soul?"

GRANT—I'm sorry, Mr. Hildebrand, but I'm just not interested in your ideas. Maybe there's something in what you say. Maybe I ought to think a little more about religion. But right now I've got a stockholder's report to get out, and that's more important than anything you can tell me. Some of these days, when I haven't anything else to do, I'll listen to you. Right now you can do me the most good by leaving me alone.

HILDEBRAND—Just as you say. But I don't intend to stop trying. Your soul may not mean much to you, but it does to me and I'll get you to see it my way yet.

GRANT—Well, you're wasting your time, but there's no law against trying. Will you tell my secretary to come in here, on your way out?

HILDEBRAND—Of course. Good day, Mr. Grant.

GRANT—Good-by, Mr. Hildebrand. [*Exit. Secretary enters.*] Miss Johnson, don't let that fellow past you again. He makes me creepy with his talk about souls and things.

MISS JOHNSON—I'm sorry, sir. I thought you might want to see him.

GRANT—Well, I don't. I haven't been inside a church for years, and he hasn't much chance of getting me inside one, either. Have you got those reports?

MISS JOHNSON—Yes, sir. Here they are. [*Singing of "The Church in the Wildwood" begins and continues rather faintly until end of scene.*]

GRANT—Hm. They look pretty good. I guess you'd better run off fifty copies of each report.

MISS JOHNSON—Yes, sir. Will there be anything else, sir?

GRANT—Yes. Where's that singing coming from?

MISS JOHNSON—There are some boys down in the court-yard. Shall I tell them to stop?

GRANT—Yes—no, wait a minute. It sounds like they're singing "The Church in the Wildwood." Strange that they should be singing that just after Mr. Hildebrand was here. I used to attend a little church out in the country. I wonder what it looks like now.

MISS JOHNSON—It may not be there any more.

GRANT—It must be there [*musing*]. The little church in the vale. Miss Johnson, I'm going out and see that church right now.

MISS JOHNSON—But you can't. You've got to make your report to your stockholders.

GRANT—That can wait. This can't. What shall it profit a man if he satisfies his stockholders and loses his own peace of mind? [*Exit.*]

[*Curtain comes down and song grows louder until Scene II, when it ceases altogether.*]

SCENE II

[*In a church. Several pews or rows of chairs will suffice, although any extra scenery will add effectiveness.* GRANT *is seated in pew as though praying.* WILSON *enters.*]

WILSON [*coming forward*]—I believe you're Judson Grant.

GRANT—Mr. Wilson! I didn't know you were still minister here.

WILSON—Yes, the Lord has spared me. And it seems He's prospered you since you left this church many years ago.

GRANT—Yes, I've made money, if that's what you mean. Somehow, that doesn't seem very important right now.

WILSON—I know. I can see it in your face. You've made money, but it's cost you more than you want to admit.

GRANT—You always did understand, Mr. Wilson. Somehow, today, I had to come back and be a boy again in this little church.

WILSON—Have you forgotten what I used to teach you: "Thou shalt love the Lord thy God with all thy heart, and with all thy soul, and with all thy strength, and with all thy mind, and thy neighbor as thyself"?

GRANT—I'm afraid I haven't paid much attention to that in the last twenty years. Other things have gotten in the way.

WILSON—It isn't too late, my son. The door is always open to those who wish to enter. The Master says, "Him that cometh unto me, I will in no wise cast out."

GRANT—Do you think I can start again? Really begin again?

WILSON—Yes. This time, when you leave this little church, take Him with you. He will guide and strengthen you.

GRANT—I will. Now I know what it means to be truly rich.

[*Curtain falls and* READER *appears.*]

READER—There are thousands of Judson Grants in our country—thousands of sick souls who have forgotten the message that they learned years ago in some humble little church. Each of us can help bring back that faith into their hearts by singing this hymn and recalling to the minds of the Judson Grants the great truth and comfort that they experienced years ago. Let us all join in singing this hymn and praying for those who have forgotten the religion of the little church in the vale.

[*The congregation or the choir sings the hymn to conclude the playlet.*]

Wonderful Words of Life

Sing them over again to me,
    Wonderful words of life;
Let me more of their beauty see,
    Wonderful words of life.
        Words of life and beauty,
        Teach me faith and duty;
Beautiful words, wonderful words,
    Wonderful words of life.

Christ, the blessed One, gives to all,
    Wonderful words of life;
Sinner, list to the loving call,
    Wonderful words of life.
        All so freely given,
        Wooing us to heaven:
Beautiful words, wonderful words,
    Wonderful words of life.

Sweetly echo the gospel call,
    Wonderful words of life;
Offer pardon and peace to all,
    Wonderful words of life.
        Jesus, only Saviour,
        Sanctify forever:
Beautiful words, wonderful words,
    Wonderful words of life.

                    —*Philip P. Bliss.*

Wonderful Words of Life

CHARACTERS

READER ⸺⸺⸺⸺⸺⸺ Preferably a woman
PHILIP ⸺⸺⸺⸺ A young man who has found Christ
BOB ⸺⸺⸺⸺⸺⸺ A jaunty young fellow
MR. HARRISON ⸺⸺⸺⸺⸺ A business man
JANET ⸺⸺⸺ ⸺⸺⸺ A girl who is sour on life

COSTUMES

Early twentieth century.

MUSIC

Singers should be backstage. Eight is about the right number. Every one may join in the singing at the end.

SETTING

[An office with two desks and chairs. Tables and other office accessories may be used.]

READER—One of the great miracles of modern times is the Bible. This Book, written by many authors at different times, has survived the attack of centuries. Today it is the leading best seller throughout the world.

Philip P. Bliss, one of America's hymn writers, supplies the answer to this astounding popularity in his hymn, "Wonderful Words of Life." It would be hard to find another phrase that so adequately describes the Bible and its message. It contains words that live and words that make men alive with spiritual vitality. There is really no mystery about the continued popularity of this Book. It supplies a strength that no other words can give to a truth-seeking soul.

Over and over in the history of the church, the Bible has shown that it contains wonderful words of life. All Sunday-school work, all personal soul-saving, to possess any power, must be based on the Word of God. Even in the world of business the Bible speaks and saves. Let us see how a young man by the name of Philip put these wonderful words to work.

[*The curtain rises, showing* PHILIP *seated at desk.* BOB *saunters in.*]

BOB—Well, if it isn't little Philip, awake and at work so early in the morning. I don't know how you manage to work so hard and still stay as happy as you do.

PHILIP—How are you feeling, Bob?

BOB—Terrible. How about telling me your secret?

PHILIP—All right. I will tell you, because I do have a system for keeping cheerful.

BOB—Don't tell me that you've discovered a new kind of patent medicine.

PHILIP—No, my remedy for trouble is an old one. I simply read my Bible every day before I come down to work, and every evening when I go home.

BOB—Read your Bible! You mean that keeps you in good humor?

PHILIP—Certainly. The Bible contains words of life, Bob. After I've read it, the little things that used to worry me at work seem too trivial to bother with. You really ought to try it for a month.

BOB—Aw, I'm not the religious kind, I guess. It wouldn't work for me.

PHILIP—It might if you tried it. Why don't you?

BOB—Aw, I don't know. Say, here comes the boss. I'd better get to work. He looks like he's in a bad mood today.

PHILIP—Better think over what I told you.

BOB—Yeah; maybe I will. [*Exit.*]

[MR. HARRISON *enters. He is a typical business man, and he seems in a bad mood.*]

PHILIP—Good morning, Mr. Harrison.

MR. HARRISON—What! Oh, good morning, Philip.

PHILIP—You don't look so well, Mr. Harrison. Something worrying you?

MR. HARRISON—It's none of your business. Oh, I'm sorry, Philip. I guess I'm just unnerved.

PHILIP—That's all right. I thought I might be of some help.

MR. HARRISON—I don't think anybody can help me with this. Still, I've got to tell somebody or I'll go crazy. You see, Philip, I've worked hard at this business for the last twenty years, and I haven't made any too much money. Now I've got a chance to make a fortune in a short time. A good chance, at that.

PHILIP—That doesn't sound like much of a problem, Mr. Harrison.

MR. HARRISON—Well, you see, this deal isn't exactly honest, but I don't believe any one could prove I was dishonest. There you are. Somehow I can't make up my mind to take the chance. Guess I'd better talk it over with a lawyer.

PHILIP—I think I have a better plan, Mr. Harrison. When I get into a difficult situation which I can't figure out myself, I generally get the answer to my problem from this Book here.

Mr. Harrison—Hm. Sounds mighty handy. What is it?

Philip—The Bible.

Mr. Harrison—What! Now look here, Philip, I don't want to be preached to. If you haven't any better advice to offer—

Philip—Suppose you try this, Mr. Harrison. It says here [*opening Bible*]: "What shall it profit a man if he gain the whole world and lose his own soul?" Or, "What shall a man give in exchange for his soul?" Doesn't that help a bit?

Mr. Harrison—Say—gain the world and lose his own soul—I never thought of that. That's an angle I missed. By George, those are wonderful words! Gain the whole world.

Philip—The whole Book is full of wonderful words, Mr. Harrison.

Mr. Harrison—Maybe I ought to look into this. I might learn more about running my business than I think. May I borrow your Bible for a while?

Philip—Surely. I have two in my desk here. Take this one.

Mr. Harrison—Thanks, Philip. You certainly took a load off my mind. [*Exit, humming and leafing through the Book. Bob enters.*]

Bob—Say, was that the boss humming like that?

Philip—That's right.

Bob—You must use mirrors or something. How in the world did you put him in such good humor in a hurry?

Philip—You may not believe it, but I put him to work, reading his Bible.

Bob—You mean the boss is going to start reading just like you do?

Philip—He's at it now.

BOB—Boy, you've almost got me convinced. Say, here comes Janet, looking downhearted. If you can cheer her up, you'll have me convinced.

PHILIP—It's worth trying. [*Enter* JANET, *looking very disconsolate.*] Hello, Janet, what's the matter with you?

BOB—Yeah, you look like you lost the rent money or something.

JANET—Quit trying to spread any good cheer my way. I've got troubles that would make losing the rent money a pleasure.

PHILIP—Suppose you tell us your troubles. That may help.

JANET—Well, it won't make them any worse. To begin with, my best beau has another girl. Then I had a fight with my father and, to top it all off, I'm to be laid off at the end of the week. There you are. I wish I were dead.

BOB—Well, Phil, start spreading the sweetness and light.

JANET—You fellows can't do anything to make me feel any better.

PHILIP—No, we can't do a thing. But listen to this, Janet, and see what you say. "Why art thou cast down, O my soul, and why art thou disquieted within me? Hope thou in God; for I shall yet praise him who is the health of my countenance and my God." [*Reads from Bible.*] Have you forgotten that there's a God to hope and trust in?

JANET—Yeah—I guess I did forget. Say, that's kind of funny, me thinking the whole world was ruined, and I'll bet God's got a lot worse cases than mine to handle.

PHILIP—You're probably right, there.

JANET—Hope thou in God. Say, those are wonderful words. Guess I was just making a fool of myself over a few troubles. Next time, I'll look to see if the Bible's got anything to help me.

PHILIP—You won't be disappointed.

JANET—Well, good-by, Bob and Phil. I've got to get to work. And thanks very much. [*Exit.*]

PHILIP—Well?

BOB—You don't need to say anything more. I'm convinced that the Bible is full of wonderful words. What do you say we read it together every day.

PHILIP [*takes him by the hand*]—That suits me fine, Bob. We'll study the wonderful words together.

[*Curtain comes down and choir sings first stanza of song. This may be omitted if desired, and the whole song sung at the end.*]

READER—And so Bob came to know the truth and glory of the Bible, and Philip spread the Word to three people that day. What happened to these men and this woman can happen to any one who will sincerely read and seek to find life in the Bible. Philip Bliss's song is an invitation to every Christian and seeker after truth to read these wonderful words and let them sink into his heart. Let us all join in singing the remaining stanzas of this great hymn.

[*Audience sings.*]

I Love to Tell the Story

I love to tell the story
   Of unseen things above,
Of Jesus and His glory,
   Of Jesus and His love;
I love to tell the story
   Because I know 'tis true;
It satisfies my longings
   As nothing else can do.

I love to tell the story:
   More wonderful it seems
Than all the golden fancies
   Of all my golden dreams;
I love to tell the story:
   It did so much for me;
And that is just the reason
   I tell it now to thee.

I love to tell the story:
   'Tis pleasant to repeat
What seems, each time I tell it,
   More wonderfully sweet;
I love to tell the story,
   For some have never heard
The message of salvation
   From God's own holy Word.

I love to tell the story,
   For those who know it best,
Seem hungering and thirsting
   To hear it like the rest;
And when, in scenes of glory,
   I sing the new, new song,
'Twill be the old, old story
   That I have loved so long.

Catherine Hankey.

I Love to Tell the Story

CHARACTERS

COSTUMES

Modern.

MUSIC

May be furnished completely by characters in play if desired, or a choir offstage may sing between the scenes.

SCENE I

[*Living-room. Chairs in a semicircle. Table and chair in center.*]

READER—Did you ever finish singing a hymn and then wonder what the words meant? That is one of the common experiences of all Christians, because we don't always consider the meaning of the words. Sometimes the hymn is so familiar that we simply sing it mechanically. Other times we are too anxious to follow the correct tune and we forget about the words. Yet most of our hymns contain real Christian messages that we would do well to consider. And in some songs we make statements that we might not be able to make if we weighed the meaning of our words. Such a hymn is "I Love to Tell the Story."

Written by Catherine Hankey and William G. Fischer, the stanzas speak of the joy and eagerness of the singer to witness for Christ. Yet, how many people really mean that when they sing "I Love to Tell the Story"? How many people really do enjoy speaking to their neighbor about his soul's salvation? Let me tell you the amazing results that occurred when one young woman came to realize what she was singing. Margaret Summers was a member of a small and struggling Christian church. One afternoon at the meeting of the Ladies' Aid Society, the opening hymn was "I Love to Tell the Story." The scene opens with the singing of the last stanza of the hymn.

[*Women are seated in a semicircle, the chairman at a table in the center. They finish singing the last stanza of the hymn.*]

CHAIRMAN—Well, ladies, I believe we are ready to begin our meeting. Shall we have the secretary's report?

MARGARET—May I say something first, Madam Chairman?

CHAIRMAN—Why, certainly, Margaret.

MARGARET—I'd like to object to the singing of that hymn at our meetings any more.

CHAIRMAN—But, Margaret, "I Love to Tell the Story" is one of our favorite songs. We've sung it many times before this.

MARGARET—I know we have. And that's just the reason I'm objecting to our singing it again.

MRS. HENDERSON—What do you mean?

MARGARET—I don't think anybody here realized what we were saying. I didn't until we got to that last verse. But, ladies, we were singing about how much we love to tell people of Jesus and His love.

CHAIRMAN—Why shouldn't we sing that?

MARGARET—Because we don't really mean it at all. I don't think there's one of us who really loves to tell the story. Just look at the small group we have here today! If we had really been interested in telling others about Jesus, I don't see how we could fail to have more people here this afternoon.

MRS. HENDERSON—Why, Margaret Summers, I don't think you ought to talk like that.

MARGARET—Maybe not, but let me ask just one question. Did any one of you during the past month actually speak to an outsider about Jesus?

[*Silence. Finally* MRS. RATHBERT *speaks.*]

MRS. RATHBERT—I invited my next door neighbor to come to church with me one Sunday. Is that what you mean we should do?

MARGARET—That's better than nothing, but did anybody really tell the story of our Saviour who died for our sins? [*Silence.*] That's what I thought. Madam Chairman, I suggest that we omit "I Love to Tell the Story" from our list of songs until we can sing it and really mean what we're saying.

CHAIRMAN [*undecided*]—Well—it's rather a strange suggestion.

MRS. JONES—I think she's right, Madam Chairman. But I don't think we should stop singing the song. I suggest that each one of us during the next month speak to some one about Jesus, and show him why he should come to our church and learn more about Him. I'm sure we could all do that, and then we could sing the song again at our next meeting.

MRS. HENDERSON—But whom could we speak to? I don't know any one who isn't a church member.

MRS. JONES—How about the woman who helps you clean on Fridays and Saturdays? Did you ever ask her about her faith?

MRS. HENDERSON—Well—no, I guess not.

MARGARET—There you are. Every one of us can do it. We can find lots of people in this community who haven't heard the story of Jesus.

CHAIRMAN—I think that is an excellent idea. It won't hurt any of us to try to win a soul for Christ, and it may prove a wonderful blessing to many people. Are you all willing to try Margaret's plan?

ALL—Yes.

CHAIRMAN—Then I guess we are finally ready to proceed with the reading of the minutes from our last meeting.

[*The curtain falls or the lights go out on the scene and the choir sings the first stanza of the song, after which the* READER *appears.*]

SCENE II

[*A plain but comfortable living-room.*]

READER—And so this small group of Christians began to take this hymn seriously and to tell their neighbors the story of Christ. They didn't find it as hard a task as they thought. For example, there was Mrs. Henderson, who finally got up enough courage to speak to Susan, who helped her with her housework. Let's see what happened.

[*The curtain rises, showing* SUSAN *busy dusting the room.* MRS. HENDERSON *enters.*]

Mrs. Henderson—Susan, can you stop a moment? I want you to sit down and talk for a little while.

Susan—Oh, all right. I was just about finished with this room anyway.

Mrs. Henderson—It's rather hard for me to say what I want to say. But you've worked for me for about three years, haven't you?

Susan—Yes, ma'am. And I hope my work has been satisfactory. I've always tried to do my best. If there's anything wrong, please tell me and I'll try to do better.

Mrs. Henderson—Why, Susan, what would make you think I wasn't satisfied with your work?

Susan—Well, this is the first time you ever sat down and talked to me like this, and I thought maybe something was wrong. I don't want to lose my job, because I need the work so badly.

Mrs. Henderson—I'm not worried about your work. But I've never asked you anything about—about your soul in all those three years, Susan. Tell me, do you go to church?

Susan—No, ma'am, I haven't for a long while.

Mrs. Henderson—Don't you ever think about Jesus and your soul and things like that?

Susan—Oh, yes. Sometimes I get pretty worried, but I never had anybody to talk to me about such things and I don't understand them myself.

Mrs. Henderson—Well, Susan, maybe I can help a little. You see, none of us is perfect in this world. We all sin and do evil things in God's sight.

Susan—I know that much, ma'am. I don't do all I should, that's certain.

Mrs. Henderson—None of us does. But God wants us all to love Him and do that which is pleasing in His sight. And so He sent His only Son into the world to pay the penalty for our sins so we could be free. And Jesus Christ died on the cross just to show that God has forgiven us and taken away our sins.

SUSAN—Did He do that for me, too?

MRS. HENDERSON—For all of us, Susan. The Bible tells us that God loved the whole world, and that anybody who believes on Christ can have eternal life.

SUSAN—Oh, that's wonderful. Why didn't you tell me this before?

MRS. HENDERSON—I guess I've been selfish with the truth. But I'll never be any more. Susan, do you want to believe in Jesus and know more about Him?

SUSAN—Oh, yes, yes, of course.

MRS. HENDERSON—Then will you go to church with me next Sunday and hear the Word of God?

SUSAN—You mean sit right beside you in church? Oh, Mrs. Henderson, I don't have any good clothes to wear, and I'd make you ashamed to be seen with me.

MRS. HENDERSON—No, Susan, Jesus didn't die just for the well-to-do, but for everybody. The poor people were His best friends. You'll make me very happy if you'll come with me so that we can both learn more about His Word.

SUSAN—I'll be there, Mrs. Henderson. And thank God you spoke to me like this today.

[*Curtain. The choir sings a stanza of the song, preferably the third. Then the* READER *appears.*]

READER—Thus a new soul was won for Christ, and Mrs. Henderson learned what it meant really to tell the story to those that had never heard. Her experience was repeated in the lives of the other members of the Ladies' Aid. Some called on their friends and for the first time made a plain statement of their faith. Others got in touch with neighbors or relatives and told them the story of Jesus. When the Ladies' Aid held their next meeting, there was a new spirit in the air.

SCENE III

[*A scene such as Scene I, but with a number of new members present. As the curtain rises, there should be a great deal of talking and visiting. The following speeches stand out above the general talk.*]

CHAIRMAN—I believe we have more people here this afternoon than we have ever had before.

MRS. RATHBERT—Yes, and wasn't the church crowded Sunday! It looked grand to see so many new faces. And it made me happy to think that I had been able to bring two new people there myself.

MRS. JONES—It's a wonderful feeling to know that the Lord has used you in that way.

MRS. HENDERSON—I should say! And to think that I was so afraid and so sure that I could never speak to any one about his soul. I think we owe Margaret Summers a vote of thanks. It was she who started us off on the right path.

MARGARET—Nonsense! I wasn't any better than the rest of you. I just suddenly realized what that hymn meant. But I think we should all start our meeting by singing "I Love to Tell the Story."

CHAIRMAN—You're sure we have a right to sing it now, Margaret?

MARGARET—Yes, and I think we're all going to keep on being able to sing it—and this time mean every word of the song.

[*The curtain falls on the singing of the first stanza of the hymn. At the conclusion of the stanza, the* READER *appears.*]

READER—There are in America alone over seventy million people who haven't heard the story of Jesus Christ or, at least, have forgotten what it means to live and walk with their Lord. We can't reach all of these people ourselves, but each one of us can help by telling others about the glorious message of the gospel. We really have no right to sing "I Love to Tell the Story" until we have done something about the unchurched seventy million in America, but let us join in singing the last two verses of the hymn tonight and let us resolve to make its words come true in our lives in the weeks and months to follow. Then, truly, " 'Twill be our theme in glory, to tell the old, old story of Jesus and His love."

[*The audience joins in singing the song.*]

Just As I Am

Just as I am! without one plea,
But that Thy blood was shed for me,
And that Thou bidd'st me come to Thee,
    O Lamb of God, I come! I come!

Just as I am! and waiting not
To rid my soul of one dark blot,
To Thee, whose blood can cleanse each spot,
    O Lamb of God, I come! I come!

Just as I am! tho' tossed about
With many a conflict, many a doubt,
With fears within, and foes without,
    O Lamb of God, I come! I come!

Just as I am! poor, wretched, blind—
Sight, riches, healing of the mind,
Yea, all I need, in Thee to find—
    O Lamb of God, I come! I come!

Just as I am! Thou wilt receive,
Wilt welcome, pardon, cleanse, relieve;
Because Thy promise I believe,
    O Lamb of God, I come! I come!

Just as I am! Thy love unknown
Has broken ev'ry barrier down;
Now to be Thine, yea, Thine alone,
    O Lamb of God, I come! I come!

—*Charlotte Elliott.*

Just As I Am

CHARACTERS

CHARLOTTE ELLIOTT { An attractive young girl who is an invalid

HARRY ELLIOTT _____Charlotte's father

EDITH ELLIOTT _____ Her mother

CÆSAR MILAN_____A minister

COSTUMES

In keeping with early nineteenth century.

SCENE I

[*The Elliott home about 1821.* CHARLOTTE *is seated on a settee, has a shawl or afghan wrapped around her; one hand plays nervously with a handkerchief. Is in deep thought.* MR. ELLIOTT *is reading the paper.*]

MR. ELLIOTT [*looks at* CHARLOTTE]—Why the lonesome look?

CHARLOTTE—Oh, I don't know—guess I was thinking—but what about is more than I know. Life is lonesome, anyway.

MR. ELLIOTT—Now, now, Daughter, that is no way to talk. We have . . .

CHARLOTTE—Please, Father, don't give me one of those sermons on being grateful. I'm not, and why pretend?

MR. ELLIOTT—I was only going to say that I wish your mother and I were as much joy to you as you are to us.

45

CHARLOTTE—Joy? Huh! Don't try to make me feel that I am of any use in this world. I am not and I know it.

[MRS. ELLIOTT *enters. Picks up sewing and sits down in a small rocking chair.*]

MRS. ELLIOTT—What is this all about? Charlotte, you were being very emphatic about what you know, whatever it is.

CHARLOTTE—Oh, just one of my old grievances, I suppose. Father thinks I should believe that every life is for some purpose.

MRS. ELLIOTT—It is, and . . .

CHARLOTTE—Now don't try to convince me that I am of any use. I am grateful to you and Father for trying to cheer me. I appreciate your love and devotion, but what is there in life for me?

MR. ELLIOTT—If there were only some way I could convince you that the sooner you become interested in something in life, the sooner you will forget that you no longer can lead an active life.

CHARLOTTE—Father, I have tried to look at it from every angle. I realize many others have been ill and later had to lead the life of an invalid. I'll admit at times I feel very much ashamed of myself because I haven't determination enough to accept my lot and at least try to be of some use to humanity. I'm a weakling . . .

MRS. ELLIOTT—My dear, that is not true. Your father and I can not see the reason either, and it makes us very sad, but all has been done within human power. I believe that when we have reached our extremity without desired results there is a reason.

CHARLOTTE—Perhaps it is peace and contentment I am seeking. My thoughts are always in a turmoil, and I can find no reason for it.

MR. ELLIOTT—There is a way, you know, that we can find peace if we only accept it.

CHARLOTTE—Yes, Mother and Mr. Milan have insisted many times that if I were to come to Christ I would be acquiring peace and at the same time doing my duty.

MR. ELLIOTT—If we could only get you to see that fact!

CHARLOTTE—If Christ wants us to accept Him, why does He made it so hard for us?

MRS. ELLIOTT—He doesn't. Any one can accept Him by simply launching out on faith.

CHARLOTTE—That may be true for some, but for me I find it very hard. Oh, well, let's talk of something else.

[*A knock is heard at the door.* MRS. ELLIOTT *rises and walks toward the door.*]

CHARLOTTE—If that is the preacher, I am not at home. [*Attempts to rise.*] Will I never remember that I can no longer walk?

[MRS. ELLIOTT *opens the door and* MR. MILAN *enters. She shakes hands with him.*]

MRS. ELLIOTT—How do you do, Mr. Milan, come right in. We are so happy to see you.

MR. MILAN—I was just passing and thought I would drop in for a moment. [*Shakes hands with* CHARLOTTE.] And how are you today, Charlotte? It seems you are looking better every time I see you.

CHARLOTTE—Thank you.

MR. MILAN [*shakes hands with* MR. ELLIOTT]—Reading the news?

MR. ELLIOTT—Yes, we seldom see a paper and they are a real treat when we do.

MR. MILAN—Indeed they are. However, I suspect they will be quite a common thing some day. Perhaps in another twenty-five years; or maybe sooner.

MR. ELLIOTT—That would be a fine thing, but it is almost too much to hope for.

MR. MILAN—We have so many pleasures now, one more isn't too much to hope for, is it? [*Smiles.* CHARLOTTE *turns head in disgust as the word "pleasure" is mentioned.*] We have so many good things in life, we should be ashamed ever to be discontented.

MR. ELLIOTT—Always something to be thankful for, isn't there?

MR. MILAN—Mrs. Elliott, I just came from Mrs. Dent's home. She is improving. She asked me to tell you she would enjoy having you visit her soon.

MRS. ELLIOTT—I'm so glad she is recovering. She has been so ill for a long time and yet remains so cheerful.

MR. MILAN—Indeed she has. You will never find her "light hid under a bushel."

CHARLOTTE—In other words, most people are not complainers as I am?

MR. MILAN—Why, Charlotte, you are not a complainer. You think worse of yourself than any one else does.

CHARLOTTE—Life is so mixed up; it seems I can't find peace and contentment in anything. Life itself is so difficult; everything in it that is worth while is made so hard to attain. All of my prejudice toward life does not come from the fact that I am an invalid.

MR. MILAN—You make things hard for yourself. God can use you if you will only let Him.

CHARLOTTE—Don't talk to me about religion. There is nothing in life for me, and if there were, it is too hard for me.

MR. MILAN—Charlotte, answer me this question: Is anything too hard for any of us to accomplish if we have help?

CHARLOTTE [*hesitatingly*]—Perhaps not. Anything as hard to live as the Christian life is too hard for me, however. Father and Mother were trying to convince me before you came in that I have the wrong outlook on life. No, Mr. Milan, there is no use to discuss it further.

MR. MILAN—Christianity is not a hard thing to acquire.

CHARLOTTE—I wish I could believe that.

MR. MILAN—If you loved some one who loved you, and that person had made a great sacrifice for you, would you find it hard to have faith in that person?

CHARLOTTE—No.

MR. MILAN—Would you find it hard to do whatever that person asked, providing it was right?

CHARLOTTE—Perhaps not.

MR. MILAN—You wouldn't question the person's reason for asking you but would grant it because you wanted to.

CHARLOTTE—But what has all this to do with me?

MR. MILAN—Just this: Christ loves you and gave His life on the cross for you. He offers you peace and happiness if you only confess Him and give Him your life. This certainly proves His great love for you as well as for all of us. Do you agree with me?

CHARLOTTE—Yes, I'll have to admit that I do.

MR. MILAN—Then why can't you come to Christ? You will be much happier.

CHARLOTTE [*speaks in a softer and more interested tone.*] Mr. Milan, I believe that I see what you mean, but I don't know where to begin. I've thought of it so often, but so many things confuse me. [*Weeps softly.*]

MR. MILAN—Now, Charlotte, you tell me what confuses you and maybe I can help you.

CHARLOTTE—I really don't know. There is so much I should do before I become a Christian—so much I must make right—and on and on my mind travels. I don't know where to begin nor what to do.

MR. MILAN—Don't try that method; cut the cable. It will take too long to unloose it. It is a small loss anyway, and you must come to Christ just as you are, trusting in His great love and power to set all things right.

CHARLOTTE—Just as I am, you say?

MR. MILAN—Yes, just as you are, and Christ will supply all that you lack. He will set your mind at rest, and you can see clearly then your path of duty.

CHARLOTTE [*in tears*]—I will give Him my life, broken though it is, trusting in His grace and power to guide me in whatever path He sees fit.

MR. MILAN—I am so happy that at last you have come to this decision. I know you will never regret it.

MRS. ELLIOTT—Oh, Charlotte, how we have prayed for you to take this step! I am sure Christ can use you in a very definite way.

MR. ELLIOTT—Words can not express the joy this brings to me to know that you will now be so much happier. Mr. Milan, we can never thank you enough for bringing about this decision.

MR. MILAN—I share your happiness, and I am sure the angels in heaven have been made to rejoice. I am sure you will be a great inspiration to many. Christ has a use for every one of us.

CHARLOTTE—Even an invalid?

MR. MILAN—Yes, even an invalid. There are no invalids in the eyes of God, so far as His using us for good is concerned. Let us pray.

[MR. and MRS. ELLIOTT *and* MR. MILAN *kneel in prayer.* CHARLOTTE *bows head.*]

CURTAIN

SCENE II

[*The* ELLIOTT *home twelve years later.* CHARLOTTE *sits reading her Bible. A portrait of Christ in the Garden stands on the table, where it can be seen by the audience.*]

CHARLOTTE [*reads*]—"Come unto me all ye that are weary and heavy laden and I will give you rest." How I should like to proclaim that message to the world, for it has meant so much to me during the years I have been a Christian. [*Looks at picture.*] Dear Jesus, you, too, were weary at times, but how I do thank Thee for the peace and comfort I have had since I accepted Thee, just as I was! [*Turns leaves of the Bible as if looking for something. Finds piece of paper and unfolds it. Smiles. A knock is heard at the door.*] Come in.

[MR. MILAN *enters.*]

MR. MILAN—Good morning, Charlotte. Are you alone?

CHARLOTTE—Yes, Mother has gone on one of her errands of mercy.

MR. MILAN [*smiles*]—Always busy helping some one, isn't she?

CHARLOTTE—Mother never seems to tire of helping others, but that is our mission in life—to do whatever good we can.

MR. MILAN—How true, but so few have that philosophy of life!

CHARLOTTE—There was a time when I was blinded to the good accomplished by even the small acts of kindness.

MR. MILAN—I am so glad those days are gone forever.

CHARLOTTE—Many times I have regretted the rude way in which I treated you at times.

MR. MILAN—That is all forgiven and forgotten, too.

[MRS. ELLIOTT *enters. Has letter in her hand.*]

MRS. ELLIOTT—Good morning, Mr. Milan. I am so glad you were here to keep Charlotte company.

MR. MILAN [*smiles*]—Yes, Charlotte and I have much more in common to talk about than we used to.

MRS. ELLIOTT [*sits down near* CHARLOTTE]—How true that is! Did you think I had forsaken you, Charlotte? I expected to be back sooner but was detained.

CHARLOTTE—No, Mother, I was reading and had hardly noticed that the time was passing so rapidly.

MRS. ELLIOTT—What have you in your hand?

CHARLOTTE—Oh, nothing. [*Hesitates.*] I was reading the Bible and happened to think of the little poem I had written a long time ago and I was just reading it over.

MRS. ELLIOTT [*excitedly*]—I have a surprise for you.

CHARLOTTE—For me?

MRS. ELLIOTT—Yes, you. That very poem which you are reading Mr. Bradbury has set to music and it is being published.

CHARLOTTE [*in astonishment*]—Mother, do you mean that?

MRS. ELLIOTT—Every word of it. Isn't it true, Mr. Milan?

CHARLOTTE—And you knew about it, too. But how did it happen?

MRS. ELLIOTT—Well, you remember the day we were preparing for the bazaar at the church?

CHARLOTTE—Yes, that was the day I wrote this poem. I was a little depressed that day because I couldn't help at the church. My thoughts drifted back to the day that Mr. Milan told me to come to Christ just as I was, and I thought how happy I had been since then. I wished that I could proclaim to the entire world that message to come to Christ just as we are.

MR. MILAN—There is undoubtedly a need in this old world for such a message. Many, many depressed souls are trying to find peace and know not how. They are doing just what you did; they are making something very hard out of what in reality is something very simple.

CHARLOTTE—But what I want to know is, how did you get the poem and how did Mr. Bradbury get it?

MRS. ELLIOTT—That is what I started to tell you. You recall I came over from the church during the afternoon of the bazaar to tell you how we were getting along, and you showed me a copy of the poem. Well, I took a copy of it without your knowledge and when Mr. Bradbury saw it he wanted to set it to music, which he did. It has now been sent to the publisher. The whole world may now not only read, but sing its message.

CHARLOTTE [*in tears*]—I am so happy, for maybe I shall not have lived in vain.

MR. MILAN—Are you convinced that Christ can use every one of us if we but trust Him?

CHARLOTTE [*smiles*]—Even an invalid.

MR. MILAN—Yes, as I told you twelve years ago, even an invalid. I am confident many souls will be shown the way of salvation by the singing of this song.

MRS. ELLIOTT—Would you like to hear it sung, Charlotte?

CHARLOTTE—Oh, yes, Mother, please.

[MRS. ELLIOTT *seats herself at the piano and begins to play. Song is sung offstage. An organ in harmony with the early nineteenth century may be used instead of the piano if one is obtainable.*]

CURTAIN

Living for Jesus

Living for Jesus a life that is true,
Striving to please Him in all that I do,
Yielding allegiance, gladhearted and free,
This is the pathway of blessing for me.

Chorus

O Jesus, Lord and Saviour,
  I give myself to Thee;
For Thou, in Thy atonement,
  Didst give Thyself for me;
I own no other master,
  My heart shall be Thy throne,
My life I give, henceforth to live,
  O Christ, for Thee alone.

Living for Jesus, who died in my place,
Bearing on Calv'ry my sin and disgrace,
Such love constrains me to answer His call,
Follow His leading and give Him my all.

Living for Jesus wherever I am,
Doing each duty in His holy name,
Willing to suffer affliction or loss,
Deeming each trial a part of my cross.

Living for Jesus thro' earth's little while,
My dearest treasure, the light of His smile,
Seeking the lost ones He died to redeem,
Bringing the weary to find rest in Him.

—*T. O. Chisholm.*

—Used by permission of Rodeheaver,
Hall-Mack Co., copyright owner.

Living for Jesus

CHARACTERS

READER	A young girl
FRED	A boy of twelve
FATHER	Kindly man
DR. BLAKE	Young, serious doctor
MRS. BLAKE	Patient wife
DR. HARTSELL	Gruff and worldly
CARSON	A fat business man
BARBARA	Young and good

COSTUMES

Modern.

MUSIC

Furnished by a small choir offstage.

READER—The accusation is sometimes made that the church lives too much in the past—that it offers no practical solutions for modern problems. Perhaps there is some truth in this criticism. Often our hymns sing of the glories of the past and of the great accomplishments in Biblical times and we fail to see their modern applications. Now, we need such hymns, but we also need some that speak of our everyday problems and the way a Christian meets difficulties today. "Living for Jesus" is one of a group of modern hymns that carry living messages to believers today. Written by T. O. Chisholm and Harold Lowden, the perfect blending of words and music in this song has quickly found its way into our hearts.

Sometimes Christians are called upon to give up their lives for the faith, and we honor their heroism. But most of us will never face that difficulty. We have to learn how to live from day to day and remain faithful to our Master. And this may prove to be an even more difficult task than to die the death of a martyr. That is why "Living for Jesus" has such a tremendous message for us today. It throws out a challenge to our souls.

Let me show you how a boy by the name of Fred Hobart learned from his father the importance of living for Jesus.

SCENE I

[*The scenes between the father and son should be played at the side of the stage away from the* READER, *either in front of the curtain or, at least, completely out of the setting so that a scene change can be made.* FRED *is seated in a chair or on the steps, reading a book. The* FATHER *enters.*]

FATHER—Hello, Son. What are you reading?

FRED—A very good book, Dad. It's all about the Christian church when it was new. My Sunday-school teacher gave it to me to read.

FATHER—Well, I'm glad to see you reading something worth while. Is the book interesting?

FRED—I'll say. There are some pretty keen stories in it. Only now and then I get to feeling bad about the way Christian people were treated back in those days. They had to suffer and do all sorts of things to be able to keep on being Christians. I guess they just had better Christians then than they do now.

FATHER—I don't know about that, Son. What would give you that idea?

FRED—Why, some of these people I'm reading about now were tortured and finally eaten by lions, but they wouldn't give up their faith. People don't have to do that to be Christians today. It's easier now.

FATHER—Thank the Lord we don't have persecution in this country. But, Fred, did you ever think that it might be just as hard to live for Christ as to die for Him?

FRED—I don't see how that can be. Nobody wants to be thrown to the lions or be burned up.

FATHER—No, but it also takes Christian strength to do some other things. Let me tell you about a few modern Christian heroes that I happen to know. First, there's my friend, Dr. Blake. He and I went to school together. Now he's practicing medicine in a small western town.

SCENE II

[*The curtain rises on the center of the stage, revealing a small office. * FRED *and his* FATHER *remain at the side of the stage. * DR. BLAKE *is seated in front of his desk, and his wife is straightening the office.*]

MRS. BLAKE—You look terribly tired, Henry.

DR. BLAKE—I guess I am this evening. I was up most of the night last night with Mrs. Hackett's little boy. He's terribly sick.

MRS. BLAKE—I feel so sorry for them. They're so poor. How's the old fellow that you've been going out to visit? You know the one I mean.

DR. BLAKE—The old prospector? He's getting back on his feet now. I'm glad he is. That was a long trip out there each week.

MRS. BLAKE—I don't suppose you'll ever get paid for that case.

DR. BLAKE—Not unless the old fellow strikes gold, so don't expect anything. But we'll manage somehow.

MRS. BLAKE—Yes, it seems like the Lord always takes care of us in one way or another. [*A knock on the door.*] I wonder who that is. Not another patient tonight, I hope. [DR. BLAKE *goes to the door and opens it.*]

DR. BLAKE—Why, Dr. Hartsell, come in, come in. What on earth brings you out here? I thought you were in New York.

DR. HARTSELL [*Enters. Very businesslike man*]—Hello, Henry. Hello, Mary. I'm on my way out West, and I just stopped off here between trains, so I can stay only a few minutes. [*Waves away chair offered.*] No, I haven't even time to sit down. But, Henry, I wanted to see you about that appointment to the medical research board. Why on earth did you turn down a $5,000 job like that?

DR. BLAKE—It was pretty hard, Dr. Hartsell.

DR. HARTSELL—Hard—it was crazy! Think, man, you could have gotten out of this little burg. You wouldn't have to make any midnight calls. Why, you might have become one of the great medical scientists if you had taken that position. Why did you do it?

DR. BLAKE—It's pretty hard to explain, Dr. Hartsell. But you know I've always been a Christian, and that's what made the difference. You've always laughed at me for my faith, but it was more important than that position or any other.

DR. HARTSELL—You could stay a Christian in New York, if you wanted to. What's that got to do with it?

DR. BLAKE—Just this: I came out to this little town, determined to serve these people. They don't pay me much

58

money, but they show in their hearts what my service means to them. If I left them now, I don't know whether any other doctor would ever come out here to this lonely place again. I think the Lord wants me here, and I'm going to stay.

Dr. HARTSELL—It still doesn't make sense. What made you resolve to do a silly thing like that?

Dr. BLAKE—Dr. Hartsell, a good long while ago, Jesus Christ died on a cross and freed us all from our sins. It's easy to ask why He did such a thing, but He did it because He loved us. Well, I'm doing this because I love Him and love His children in this community. I can't die for Him, as He did for me, but at least I can live for Him and sacrifice a little to do His work in this world.

CURTAIN

SCENE III

[*The choir should sing the first stanza of the hymn.*]

FRED—Say, that was a swell story. That doctor really is a Christian.

FATHER—I told you, Son, that all the faithful believers aren't dead yet. Are you convinced now that there are just as good Christians today as there ever were?

FRED—Well, partly. I guess people make a lot of sacrifices sometimes. Only people aren't persecuted today like they once were, and I think that would be the hardest thing to suffer.

FATHER—You're still holding onto that idea, eh? Well, I said I'd tell you about several people who are living for Jesus today, so suppose I tell you about Barbara Pendle. You see, Barbara is a Christian girl who works in an office.

SCENE IV

[*Curtain rises on office scene. Mr. Carson is seated behind desk and Barbara stands in front of the desk. Carson is big and gruff.*]

Carson—Miss Pendle, we've had some complaints on your work.

Barbara—Oh, Mr. Carson! I'm so sorry. I'll try to work faster in the future.

Carson—It's not the speed of your work. But Mr. Jones tells me that you refuse to obey orders at times.

Barbara—Oh, I guess he didn't tell you the whole story, then. You see, Mr. Jones asked me several times to tell people things that weren't true, and once he wanted me deliberately to overcharge a man in the hope that he wouldn't notice it and thus would pay the little extra amount.

Carson—Hum. Well, you must understand, Miss Pendle, that in business sometimes we do things that we may not necessarily approve of, but we must keep pace with our competitors.

Barbara—You mean you want me to lie and steal for the company?

Carson—I want you to obey orders, regardless of what you think of them.

Barbara—But I'm a Christian, Mr. Carson. I know it's wrong to do such things, and how can I do them, then?

Carson—You'd better be careful, or we'll be forced to get some one else in your place.

Barbara—Oh, but I need my job so badly. I don't know where I'd get another one.

Carson—I thought that would bring you around. You are willing to do what you're told, hereafter?

BARBARA—No, no, you can't threaten or bribe me into sin. Listen, Mr. Carson, I've always been a Christian and God has always protected me. His own Son died to save me from my sins. How can you expect me to turn against Him now? I'm living my life for Jesus and trying to follow His teachings. I won't change from that, no matter what it may cost.

CARSON—I'm very sorry you're so stubborn, young lady. You might have gone a long way with this company. But I'm afraid we'll have to dispense with your services. And just to see how much good your Christianity will do you, I'll not give you a letter of recommendation, either. That will be all, Miss Pendle.

CURTAIN

SCENE V

[*The choir sings the second stanza of the hymn.*]

FATHER—Well, Fred, that ought to show you that people are persecuted today, just as they once were. Maybe not with threats of physical torture, but the persecution for faith goes on, just the same.

FRED—I guess I didn't realize that, Dad. I guess maybe it costs pretty much to be a Christian nowadays, too.

FATHER—Yes, we have heroes of faith in every generation. The attacks made against Christians come in many ways. But always, if we live close to Jesus, we shall have nothing to fear from these attacks.

FRED—Thanks, Dad, for telling me this. I'm going to tell my Sunday-school teacher all about it Sunday.

FATHER—Well, right now I suspect it's supper time, so suppose we both go and get ready.

FRED—O. K. I think I can eat some supper, all right. [*They walk off the stage and the* READER *appears.*]

READER—Fred's lesson is one that we all have to learn. It is just as heroic to live a Christian life amidst hardships as to die a martyr's death. Few of us may have an opportunity to make a great display of our Christian faith, but we can at least live for Jesus by trying to do His will here on earth. The hymn, "Living for Jesus," should mean a great deal to all of us. Let us all unite in singing the last stanza of this hymn. We can sing and live for the Lord.

I Gave My Life for Thee

I gave my life for thee,
  My precious blood I shed,
That thou might'st ransomed be,
  And quickened from the dead.
I gave my life for thee;
What hast thou given for me?

I spent long years for thee,
  In weariness and woe,
That an eternity
  Of joy thou mightest know.
I spent long years for thee;
Hast thou spent one for me?

My Father's home of light,
  My rainbow-circled throne
I left for earthly night,
  For wanderings sad and lone.
I left it all for thee;
Hast thou left aught for me?

I suffered much for thee,
  More than thy tongue can tell
Of bitterest agony,
  To rescue thee from hell.
I suffered much for thee;
What canst thou bear for me?

And I have brought to thee,
  Down from my home above,
Salvation full and free,
  My pardon and my love.
Great gifts I brought to thee;
What hast thou brought to me?

—*Frances Havergal.*

I Gave My Life for Thee

CHARACTERS

JOSEPH   FREDERICK { Son of Mr. Frederick, about twenty-one years old.

FRANCES   HAVERGAL { Young woman about twenty-one years old — author of "I Gave My Life for Thee."

HENRY   FREDERICK { A minister of a church in France; a former college friend of Mr. Havergal.

MRS. ELSIE BOOK { Elderly woman who lives at the almshouse.

W. H. HAVERGAL _____Frances' father; a minister

COSTUMES

As nearly as possible, in harmony with the year 1858.

SCENE I

[*The* FREDERICK *living-room.* JOSEPH *is sitting in a comfortable chair, seemingly almost asleep. A knock is heard at the door.* JOSEPH *very suddenly sits erect as if startled by the knock, then goes to the door. Opens the door and* FRANCES *is seen standing there, attired in street clothes.*]

JOSEPH—How do you do?

FRANCES—Is Mr. Frederick in, please?

JOSEPH—No, but I think I can find him, if you would care to come in and wait.

FRANCES [*enters*]—Thank you. Perhaps he is too busy to receive callers.

JOSEPH—Oh, no, Father is never too busy to receive visitors. [*Offers her a chair.*] I am not sure that I know where he is, but I'll find him. [*Starts toward door, then turns and looks back at* FRANCES.] Are you from America?

FRANCES—Yes, I am. You see, your father and my father were college chums when they were both in ministerial training, and have been friends for years, even though they have been separated for a long time.

JOSEPH—Then I'll bet I know who you are; you are Frances Havergal.

FRANCES—That's right, but how did you guess it?

JOSEPH—Oh, Father often tells me about your father, and I remember he said that Mr. Havergal had a daughter named Frances. I also remember his telling about your mother's death. I think your father wrote him about it, although that has been some time ago, hasn't it?

FRANCES—Yes, quite a while ago. Father insisted that I come and see your father while in France. He said it would be most delightful if I saw him only a few minutes.

JOSEPH—I wish that my father had chosen America as his field of service. I don't like it here. Maybe I shouldn't like America either. I've never been there, although most of our close friends here are Americans.

FRANCES—You probably would. Every one does. But France is very beautiful. Maybe you can have the pleasure of coming to America some day. I never expected to see France, but Father thinks every one should travel and for several years had planned on my making this trip.

JOSEPH—I hope to travel, after I get through school and can make my own money. [*Smiles.*] You know as I do, perhaps, that a minister's salary doesn't allow for many trips. Here I am wasting your time talking to you when it is really Father you came to see. [*Starts toward door, looking back.*]

FRANCES—I've enjoyed talking with you. Don't forget, I'll be expecting to see you in America some day.

JOSEPH—I hope so, and it has been so pleasant meeting you. Good-by and good luck if I don't see you again. I have an appointment in a few minutes, so I must hurry. [*Exit.*]

[FRANCES *rests her head on the chair back.*]

FRANCES—My, but I am tired!

[*After a short pause, she raises her head and begins to look around at the study. Several pictures, mottoes and diplomas hang on the wall. Her gaze at last falls on a picture of Christ. Under it is the inscription, "I Gave My Life for Thee."*]

FRANCES [*rises and walks closer to picture*]—What a beautiful thought, and yet few ever think of it! [*Goes back to chair and sits down as if in meditation.*] Some one really ought to put that thought into song. Here I am going poetic again. [*Opens purse and seems to be looking for something. At last finds a circular and begins to write; then reads what she has written. Reads first verse of song, "I Gave My Life for Thee."*] Oh, that's not worth anything. I wish I had more talent in the thing that I so much enjoy doing. [*Throws paper in wastebasket. Hesitates, then takes it from basket.*] Maybe I'll save it anyway. [*Enter* MR. FREDERICK *and advances toward* FRANCES. *She rises.*]

MR. FREDERICK—And you are the daughter of my old friend, William! How glad I am to see you!

FRANCES—Yes, and I am so happy to see you. Father has talked so much about you I felt that I really knew you before I came.

Mr. Frederick—Now, my dear, tell me all about yourself and your family.

Frances—There really isn't much to tell that Father hasn't written you.

Mr. Frederick—I was very sorry, indeed, when I learned of your mother's death.

Frances—Yes, it was, of course, a shock to us all. Father is very lonely at times, more so than I. You see, Father does a remarkable job of being both mother and father to me.

Mr. Frederick—Your father is a remarkable man.

Frances—Naturally, I think so, and he is never too busy to listen to all my notions, regardless of how trivial.

Mr. Frederick—By the way, didn't I hear you reading something as I came in?

Frances [hesitates]—Oh, just one of my silly notions about trying to write poetry. That's my hobby, I guess.

Mr. Frederick—May I see what you have written? [Frances hands him the paper. He reads it, then speaks.] How beautiful—and where did you get the idea?

Frances—From the inscription under your picture of Christ.

Mr. Frederick—To be able to write poetry that well is a talent, not a hobby. That picture has been there for years, and I had never even thought of using it for a sermon.

Frances—You are just like Father—so encouraging.

Mr. Frederick—Promise me one thing, and that is when you go back you will show this to your father. If he is as talented in music as he was when we were in college, he should be able to write the music for this.

Frances—I usually show my attempts at writing to Father, and I'll promise to do the same with this one. I am sorry that I can not stay longer, Mr. Frederick, but I must in a very few moments meet the party of friends who are traveling with me. Do plan to visit us in America soon. Your son said that he was very anxious to come. [*Rises and walks closer to the door.*]

MR. FREDERICK [*shakes hands with* FRANCES]—How I wish you could stay longer and that I might see your father, but give him my kindest wishes, and good luck to you! Good-by. [FRANCES *leaves, saying "Good-by" as she goes out the door.*]

CURTAIN

SCENE II

[*An almshouse.* MRS. BOOK *is seen sewing as* FRANCES *enters.*]

MRS. BOOK—Well, well, here is my little friend. I was about to decide you had forgotten me. It has been so long since you were here, and I was almost sure that you were back from your trip to France.

FRANCES—I never forget my friends, but I have been so busy I just didn't get over. You will forgive my neglect this time, won't you?

MRS. BOOK—Of course I shall. After all, it isn't every young girl who would take time to visit an old lady in the almshouse.

FRANCES—I consider it a pleasure—I really do.

MRS. BOOK—Honey, there is one thing I want you to promise me—that you will always be the dear, sweet girl you are now. There is nothing so inspiring as a young person who shows the fine Christian attitudes you do.

FRANCES—Now don't flatter me, but if I have any admirable characteristics, I have you and my father to thank. To come to visit you is as good as going to church.

Mrs. Book—There is one thing that we must all remember, and that is, we may have little of this world's goods, but as long as we are children of God we are rich. That is one reason that I have never felt abused because I was compelled to come here. Did you bring any poetry to read to me today?

Frances—Yes, I have one little poem I have written. Frankly, I didn't think any one but you would appreciate it, for, after all, it is very simple. The thought expresses what I have heard you say many times, but I had never thought about putting it into verse. You see, while I was in France I went to see an old friend of Father's, and while waiting for him in his study I saw a picture of Christ and under it were these words: "I Gave My Life for Thee." I tried to put the thought into verse, but after writing one stanza I came near throwing it away. Then the thought came to me that you at least would like it. About that time Mr. Frederick came in, and during the conversation noticed the circular on which I had written the poem. He said that he had heard me reading when he came in and was wondering what had interested me so. Well, there was nothing else to do but tell him. He wanted me to have Father set the words to music, but I haven't. Then, coming over on the boat, I decided that you would want a longer poem than that, so I wrote another stanza. So you see I really hadn't forgotten you. [*Smiles, takes circular from purse.*]

Mrs. Book—Do read it. Since you wrote it the poem will mean more to me than one from the most talented poet.

Frances—Well, here it is. [*Reads two stanzas of the song.*]

Mrs. Book—Honey, that is beautiful! I like it better than any you have written, and the people of the world need to be more conscious of what Christ really did for them. There are a great many people who will pay more attention to the words of a song than to the greatest sermon ever preached. Now why don't you show the poem to your father and have him compose a melody for it?

FRANCES—That would be a waste of his time. There are few people in this world who see as much in the simple little thoughts as you. No, I don't think it worth while. These were merely written for your pleasure and to express what is to me a very forceful thought.

MRS. BOOK—Many great masterpieces were considered worthless by the composer. Please do what I ask you.

FRANCES—I may.

MRS. BOOK—Then do it for me. Some day when all the congregations in the large churches are singing that song I'll just smile to myself and say, "Those verses were written for my pleasure, and at least one of them was never read by any one else until I saw it." [Hesitates, half smiles.] And I an old lady in the poorhouse.

FRANCES—You are so sweet, but don't ever let me hear you refer to your being in a poorhouse. Remember the old saying, "Stone walls do not a prison make"? Well, no place you would ever be with your fine spirit would be a poorhouse.

MRS. BOOK—Thank you, my dear, for your remarks; but I am afraid that it is little good I can do any more in this world.

FRANCES—I really must be going. It will soon be supper time, and Father has a meeting at the church tonight, so I must have his supper on time. I'll not stay away so long next time, and maybe I can bring something more interesting to read to you.

MRS. BOOK—Nothing can be more interesting than what you brought today. That poem has great possibilities, and

I want you to do as I ask you; then, maybe some day when you come, you can even sing it for me. It's a promise now?

FRANCES—All right, I'll at least ask Father his opinion. Good-by. I'll see you soon. [*Exit.*]

CURTAIN

SCENE III

[*Living-room.* MR. HAVERGAL *is seated at a table, writing, as* FRANCES *enters. She has just returned from the almshouse.*]

MR. HAVERGAL—I began to think you were lost. [*Smiles.*]

FRANCES—[*Begins to straighten papers, books and other things about the room.*] Haven't you learned to look for me when you see me?

MR. HAVERGAL—It's hard to teach an old dog new tricks, you know, and I still think of you as a little girl. Seriously now, I'll bet I can make one guess where you have been.

FRANCES [*smiling*]—All right, make a guess.

MR. HAVERGAL—Over to the poorhouse to see Mrs. Book.

FRANCES—Right you are. I hadn't been over there since I came back and I knew she would be looking for me. I like to visit with her anyway. She has the sweetest philosophy of life and she is a real inspiration.

MR. HAVERGAL—You're right. She is a real Christian; never complains about her lot, either.

FRANCES—She considers herself rich in other ways than material riches, and not many of us can arrive in our thoughts to that place.

MR. HAVERGAL—She told me the other day that you frequently brought poetry to read to her. She is very fond of it; and then she added that the little verses you composed yourself were the best.

FRANCES—Yes, Mrs. Book is like you. She always lends a listening ear to my hobby of writing poetry.

MR. HAVERGAL—By the way, haven't you written any lately?

FRANCES [*smiling*]—Quite a coincidence! Mrs. Book makes me promise to show you the one I read her today and then you ask if I have written any. Yes, I have one, but thought so little of it I threw it in the wastepaper basket and then decided to save it for Mrs. Book, anyway. [*Hands paper with poem on it to* MR. HAVERGAL. *He takes paper and reads it.*]

MR. HAVERGAL—I like that very much. When did you write this?

FRANCES—While I was in France in Mr. Frederick's study waiting for him. Father, there was a picture of Christ hanging on the wall and underneath it the inscription, "I Gave My Life for Thee." I don't know why, but it impressed me very deeply. It seemed that that thought was directed at me and that Christ was challenging me to do something more for Him. It is strange how forcefully things strike us at times. I felt I must put that thought into verse, and so I wrote this first stanza; then the other I wrote on my way home. I was almost depressed, so much did I want to challenge every one to realize what Christ had done and the little we do in return! If there were only some way to make more people realize our debt, but how can that be? Seemingly preaching alone can't do it.

MR. HAVERGAL—It *is* strange how some of the very simple things inspire us.

FRANCES—Mrs. Book made me promise that I would show you this, and that maybe you could write the music to it. I don't think it worth that trouble, however. It didn't express forcefully enough what I felt, and had I not known that Mrs. Book would enjoy it I probably would never have taken it from the wastebasket.

MR. HAVERGAL—Mrs. Book has an idea there. It would make a very effective and inspiring song. Let's see if I can find a tune for it. [*Goes to piano and slowly begins picking out a few chords.*] How does this sound? [*Plays the song, "I Gave My Life for Thee."*]

FRANCES—Why, that is beautiful! Let's sing it.

[*Sing entire song. If the characters are not able to play and sing it, a duet, trio or quartet may be used.*]

CURTAIN

Nearer, My God, to Thee

Nearer, my God, to Thee,
  Nearer to Thee!
E'en though it be a cross
  That raiseth me,
Still all my song shall be,
Nearer, my God, to Thee,
Nearer to Thee!

Tho' like a wanderer,
  The sun gone down,
Darkness comes over me,
  My rest a stone;
Yet in my dreams I'd be
Nearer, my God, to Thee,
Nearer to Thee!

There let my way appear,
  Steps unto heaven:
All that thou sendest me,
  In mercy given;
Angels to beckon me,
Nearer, my God, to Thee,
Nearer to Thee!

Then, with my waking thoughts
  Bright with Thy praise,
Out of my stony griefs,
  Bethel I'll raise;
So by my woes to be,
Nearer, my God, to Thee,
Nearer to Thee!

Or if on joyful wing,
  Cleaving the sky,
Sun, moon and stars forgot,
  Upward I fly;
Still all my song shall be,
Nearer, my God, to Thee,
Nearer to Thee!

—*Sarah F. Adams.*

Nearer, My God, to Thee

CHARACTERS

READER _____A young girl
JACOB _____A young man
MERCHANT _____An elderly man
ANGELS _____ _____A number of young girls
VOICE _____ _____A deep, resonant voice
A CHOIR _____Six or eight voices (offstage)

COSTUMES

As simple as possible. Jacob needs a bright-colored robe. The merchant may wear a black robe and the angels may dress in white robes or white dresses.

SCENE I

[*Bare stage. Several large rocks are shown.*]

READER—One of the most important functions of Christian hymns is to bring comfort and strength to those who are in trouble. Many a believer in Christ has found new courage in the familiar words of a great hymn. Perhaps the most famous of these comforting songs is "Nearer, My God, to Thee." In times of danger, this is the melody that most frequently recurs to those who are menaced. When the great ocean liner "Titanic" struck an iceberg in the Atlantic Ocean, hundreds of passengers soon came to realize that they were doomed. But their hearts did not quail before their fate. The last thing that was heard before

77

the great ship plunged to its watery grave was the sound of the passengers singing, "Nearer, My God, to Thee." No finer example of the power of this hymn over the human heart could be given.

Despite its familiarity, however, few people realize that the inspiration for the words of the song is contained in the story of Jacob and the ladder he saw reaching to heaven. The poet, Sarah Adams, cleverly wove this story into verse. She managed to give it an appeal to all, for all of us, like Jacob, are wanderers in a strange land and we receive comfort from the abiding presence of God. So, let us portray for you the story of Jacob's ladder and see how the hymn fits the record of Genesis.

[*The* CHOIR *sings the first stanza of the hymn.* READER *remains in view.*]

You will remember that Jacob aroused the anger of Esau by stealing his birthright. But Rebekah, his mother, wasn't willing to see her sons quarreling, and she did not wish Jacob to marry a heathen woman. So she prevailed upon her husband to send Jacob to her home at Haran. Thus our story begins with a homesick boy traveling to his Uncle Laban's home.

[*The curtain rises, showing* JACOB *just coming on stage. The light should be dim throughout this scene.*]

JACOB [*talking to himself*]—It's getting dark, and there doesn't seem to be any place around here to stay. Not even the tent of some wild shepherd. But I guess I'll have to stay here. I'm almost too tired to go another step. [*Looks into distance.*] But, say, there comes some one. Maybe he can direct me to some shelter. [*Shouts.*] Hallo, hallo there!

MERCHANT [*comes onto stage*]—Good evening, lad. What are you doing out here in the wilderness?

JACOB—I'm traveling from Beersheba to my uncle's home in Haran. It's strange meeting some one out here. Do you live near here?

MERCHANT—No, I'm afraid not, lad. As a matter of fact, I happen to be a merchant from Haran, on my way to purchase some fine stones.

JACOB—From Haran! Then perhaps you know my Uncle Laban.

MERCHANT—Indeed I do. He's a very clever man, and you would do well to learn from him. But I don't think you can get to Haran tonight. Looks like you're going to have to sleep here in the desert.

JACOB—Aren't there any villages or houses near by?

MERCHANT—Nothing, lad. But you'll be safe here in the wilderness. No one will bother a traveler. It is the law of the desert.

JACOB—Are you traveling farther tonight?

MERCHANT—I'm afraid I must. I prefer to travel by night, when it is cool. But you'll have lots of company here. The stars will wink at you, and the moon and the wind will keep watch.

JACOB—But it's awfully lonesome. And I don't even have a pillow or anything on which to lay my head.

MERCHANT—Well, well, you want real comfort, lad. But just gather some stones here and pile them up for a pillow. I've done it often and it works very well. But I must be on my journey. Pleasant dreams, and no doubt your God will be with you. Don't let your Uncle Laban cheat you.

JACOB—Good-by, my friend. Perhaps I shall see you in Haran. [MERCHANT *exit*. JACOB *begins to pile up stones for a pillow*.] Ugh, these things are hard. I wish that merchant could have stayed. Even God Himself wouldn't be out here in this wilderness. Oh, well, there's nothing I can do about it. I might as well go to sleep. [*Lies down on rocks.*] I wonder what he meant about my Uncle Laban. [*Drops off to sleep.*]

[*Curtain. The* CHOIR *sings the second stanza of the hymn.*]

SCENE II

[*The ladder scene may be handled in several ways. Steps and platforms may be used. Several real ladders may be employed, or the angels may be varied in height to give the idea of steps to heaven. The idea is to suggest and not completely to portray the action. The lights should be dim.*]

READER [*reads from Bible*]—"And he dreamed, and behold a ladder set upon the earth, and the top of it reached to heaven, and behold the angels of God ascending and descending on it." [*The curtain rises.*]

ANGEL—Jacob, Jacob.

JACOB [*stirring in sleep but remaining in the same position*]—I see the heavens opened. And it must be angels appearing before my eyes. I must be dreaming, but it seems so real. So real.

ANGEL—It is real, Jacob. The Lord has sent you a vision to show you His will. Listen to the words of the Lord Himself, and learn how you are to be blessed.

VOICE [*The* VOICE *is offstage. It should be very loud and resonant*]—I am the Lord God of Abraham thy grandfather, and the God of Isaac; the land you are lying upon, I will give to you and to your descendants. And your descendants will be as numerous as the dust of the earth; and your people will spread abroad to the west and to the east, and to the north and to the south; and in you and in your descendants all the families of the earth will be blessed.

And lo, I am with you and will protect you in all places where you may go, and I will bring you again to this land, for I will not leave you until I have performed the things that I have promised you. [*The lights fade.* JACOB *stirs uneasily, and then the curtain comes down. The* CHOIR *sings the third stanza of the hymn.*]

READER—And so Jacob had his remarkable vision in the wilderness, the place where he thought God could not dwell. He learned that God did not desert even a homeless boy wandering in the desert. Jacob never forgot that it was impossible to escape from the presence of God.

[*The curtain rises as the lights go up on the sleeping* JACOB, *who wakes and sits up.*]

JACOB [*stretches*]—Oh, that was a hard bed. But I didn't mind it. What a wonderful dream I had! Surely the Lord is in this place, and I didn't know it. I thought God couldn't be found in a desert place. It rather frightens me. This stone seems like the house of God and the gate of heaven. At least it is for me, because God has spoken to me here. I know what I will do. I'll mark this a holy place so that I won't forget it if I come this way again. [*Begins to gather up some of the stones and constructs a rude altar.*] It's a good thing I brought some oil along, for that will serve to hallow this place. [*Takes oil flask from belt.*] What shall I name this altar? [*Muses.*] Oh, I have it. Bethel. That's it. It means the house of God. [*Pours oil on altar.*] O God, I thank you for your vision and the promise that you have made to me. I know that I haven't deserved it, for I have stolen my brother's birthright and deceived my own father. But I am sorry for my shortcomings. Forgive me. And now let me make a vow to you. If you will be with me and keep me in the journey that I am making, and will give me bread to eat and raiment to put on, so that I may come

81

to my father's house in peace, then you shall certainly be my own God, and this stone that I have set up here for a pillar shall be God's house, and of all that you will give me, surely I'll give the tenth to you. [*He drops to his knees and continues in prayer as the curtain falls slowly. The* CHOIR *sings the fourth stanza of the hymn.*]

READER—And so Jacob went on his way a changed young man. For God had shown mercy to him and assured him of protection even in a strange land. This is the story of Jacob's ladder, as recorded in the twenty-eighth chapter of Genesis. It is not hard to see how it forms the basis for our hymn, "Nearer, My God, to Thee."

Few of us receive any special revelation from God as Jacob did. We aren't permitted to see heavenly beings climbing on ladders or to hear the voice of God itself. But when we are in trouble, or are far from home, we can have the comfort as it is found in the great hymn, "Nearer, My God, to Thee." Whether we travel in the desert or in the crowded city, every step that we take brings us nearer to our God and the day we shall be with Him. Let us all join in singing the last stanza of this hymn and let its words of comfort come into our hearts. [*The whole audience may join in the singing, or, if desired the* CHOIR *may also sing the last stanza.*]

Jesus, Saviour, Pilot Me

Jesus, Saviour, pilot me
Over life's tempestuous sea;
Unknown waves before me roll,
Hiding rock and treach'rous shoal;
Chart and compass come from Thee;
Jesus, Saviour, pilot me.

As a mother stills her child,
Thou canst hush the ocean wild;
Boist'rous waves obey Thy will
When Thou say'st to them, "Be still";
Wondrous Sov'reign of the sea,
Jesus, Saviour, pilot me.

When at last I near the shore,
And the fearful breakers roar
'Twixt me and the peaceful rest,
Then, while leaning on Thy breast,
May I hear Thee say to me,
"Fear not, I will pilot thee."

—*Edward Hopper.*

Jesus, Saviour, Pilot Me

CHARACTERS

READER	Preferably a woman
EDWARD HOPPER	A minister; virile
DICK	Small sailor; young
HARRY	Big, powerful sailor
CAPTAIN	Weatherbeaten, curt
JIM	Boy on boat
MATE	Middle-aged

COSTUMES

Late nineteenth century.

MUSIC

By a choir offstage. The group should be small, chiefly women's voices.

SCENE I

[*Pastor's study. Three chairs are needed.*]

READER—Perhaps no group is so close to God's creation and power as those who toil and work on the ocean. In the roar of the waves, the fury of the storm and the calm that comes after, they can see the handiwork of the Almighty. Yet often it is a difficult task to bring the message of salvation to sailors. Their rough, hard life does not seem always to contain any place for Christ Jesus. During the last century, one of the most successful soul-winners of seafaring men was Mr. Edward Hopper. His church, located near the harbor of New York, was known as "The Church of Sea and Land." Sailors flocked to his services and many souls were saved.

While doing this work, Mr. Hopper seized upon the idea of writing a hymn that would appeal especially to those who knew and loved the sea. The idea of composing special hymns for certain types of audiences was widely used by Charles Wesley, and Mr. Hopper decided to follow the practice. So he wrote the hymn, "Jesus, Saviour, Pilot Me." This hymn was introduced in the services at "The Church of Sea and Land," and was sung enthusiastically by the sailors. But its influence reached out to Christians everywhere, and, today, all groups of believers sing "Jesus, Saviour, Pilot Me."

Perhaps the power of this great hymn can best be shown in the life of a sailor, Harry Stevens, who attended an evening service at "The Church of Sea and Land" and whose heart was touched by the singing. After the service, accompanied by a friend, he went to Mr. Hopper's study for spiritual guidance and strength.

[*Curtain rises.* MR. HOPPER *is seated at his desk. There is a knock at the door.*]

MR. HOPPER—Come in. [*Goes to door and opens it.* DICK *and* HARRY *enter.*]

DICK—Good evening, Mr. Hopper.

MR. HOPPER.—Hello, Dick. Back in port again, eh?

DICK—That's right. It's good to be back, too, and to come to the services again. But I brought a friend with me tonight, and I want you to meet him. This is Harry Stevens.

MR. HOPPER—I'm glad to know you, sir. Pull up a chair and we can get better acquainted.

HARRY—Thank you. [*They all sit down.*]

MR. HOPPER [*to Harry*]—I see you're a sailor, too.

HARRY—Off the "Jamestown," sir. But we're sailing again in the morning. Dick invited me to attend your services.

Mr. Hopper—That's fine. I'm glad you came. And are you a follower of Christ, like Dick?

Harry—Well, sir, that's kinda what I wanted to talk to you about.

Dick—I told him you could help him to decide.

Mr. Hopper—I don't suppose I'll be much help. But the Lord will guide us into all truth. What is it that bothers you, Harry?

Harry—Well, it's not easy to say. You see, I've been a sailor since I was sixteen, and I've never had any time for religion or anything like that. But, sometimes, when a fellow's out on watch at night by himself he can't help thinking about things. You know how it is.

Mr. Hopper—Yes, Harry, we can't get away from God, even out on the ocean.

Harry—That's what I mean. Seems like my way of living has just been a sort of drifting without a rudder or anything. So when Dick invited me to come along tonight, I was hoping maybe I could get a little help in the services. I enjoyed the sermon and everything, but it was that hymn about Jesus being the Pilot that seemed to fit. It made me think maybe I needed a pilot.

Mr. Hopper—We all do, Harry.

Dick—That's right, sir. That song taught me to let somebody else do the piloting for me.

Harry—It sounds good to hear you say that. But you see, I'm just not sure how to go about it. I know I don't do what I should, but just how does a fellow go about giving control over to God?

Mr. Hopper—Well, Harry, when the pilot of a boat steers, he follows a course that's been laid out for him. He can get charts and helps to guide him. And that's just what you have to do, too. God has put His chart in a book to help you. And that Book tells you that you have to be sorry for your shortcomings and try to follow the course under Jesus' guidance the best you can.

HARRY—Does that mean all the time?

MR. HOPPER—Yes, every minute. You'll have to put yourself completely under the guidance of Jesus, no matter what may happen.

HARRY—That seems pretty hard to do. Lots of the fellows on the ship would laugh at me if I told them that I was a Christian.

MR. HOPPER—Has your life been completely happy up to now, Harry?

HARRY—No—no I guess it hasn't.

MR. HOPPER—Then why not give this thing a chance? Try Jesus as your Pilot and see if He doesn't bring you the peace that you're missing.

HARRY—Well—[*Struggling with self. He should be walking the floor by this time.*]—all right, I'm willing to give it a try.

DICK—Good boy! I knew you would.

HARRY—I'm going to need lots of help and prayers. It's not so easy.

MR. HOPPER—No, it's not easy, Harry. But you'll not regret this step. You have a Friend to take with you on your voyage tomorrow. [*Opens desk and takes out a Testament.*] This will help you, too. It's a New Testament, and it will show you the way when you're not sure how your Pilot wants you to go.

HARRY—Thank you. I wonder if I could have a copy of that hymn. I'd like to learn it, if I could.

MR. HOPPER—Certainly. You may take this hymnal along. You may find some one else aboard ship that needs a Pilot, too.

HARRY—Well, thank you for everything. I guess Dick and I had better be shoving off.

MR. HOPPER—I'm so glad that you stopped. My prayers will be with you. And thanks, Dick, for bringing another soul into port.

DICK—Why shouldn't I? I know what it's done for me.

HARRY—Well, good night, sir.

DICK—Good night, Mr. Hopper.

MR. HOPPER—Good night, and God be with you both.

[*The curtain falls. The choir sings the first stanza of the hymn, after which the* READER *appears again.*]

READER—And so Harry took Jesus as his Pilot when he went aboard the "Jamestown." It wasn't easy to remain faithful, though, when his companions jibed at him for his faith. But he wasn't to be deterred, and at last there came the opportunity to show his companions what it meant to be a Christian. Our second scene opens in the captain's cabin. The "Jamestown" has run into a heavy storm.

SCENE II

[*The curtain rises, revealing a bare table with several men seated round it on weatherbeaten chairs. The* CAPTAIN *is walking back and forth.* HARRY *is seated at one side, reading his Bible. The setting should be plain and rough. A wind machine or some other device may give the storm noises, although they are not absolutely necessary.*]

CAPTAIN—Twenty years I've been captain of the "Jamestown," but she never ran into a storm like this. She's a sturdy boat, but she's an old one, too.

JIM [*frightened*]—You mean we might not pull through?

CAPTAIN—I'm not saying what I think. But I'd just as leave be out of this.

JIM—I should have stayed home, like my mom said.

CAPTAIN—Shut up your sniveling, Jim. Crying won't help none. What are you doing, Harry?

HARRY—I'm reading my Bible and praying that the Lord will pilot us through this storm.

CAPTAIN—I might have known. Ever since you came on board for this trip you've done nothing but pray and read that Book. Well, I guess it can't hurt you none, though it's not likely to do you any good, either. Mate!

MATE—Aye, aye, sir.

CAPTAIN—Go up and tell Bill to steer her south. Maybe we'll hit calmer waters that way. Won't hurt to try.

MATE—Aye, aye, sir. [Exit.]

JIM—Gee, that sounds worse, instead of better. That wind is really blowing.

CAPTAIN—If any man can pull us through, Bill can do it. He's got nerve and grit. Something you could stand a bit of, Jim.

HARRY—Give the boy time, Captain. Jim, you've got to expect a few storms in this world. But you don't have to worry if you've got the right pilot.

CAPTAIN—Now you're preaching to him, eh, Harry. Well, maybe your religion is O. K. for milksops like Jim, but not for a real man.

MATE [rushing in]—Captain, Captain, Bill's gone! Washed overboard in the storm, I guess. [They all get up and stare at him.] There's nobody at the wheel, and none of the other men'll take a chance at it. It's suicide in this storm for a man to stand up there.

CAPTAIN—But we've got to have some one at the wheel. The ship will pound against those reefs, if we don't. And Bill's gone!

MATE—Just as clean as if somebody had stolen him away.

CAPTAIN—Won't anybody take hold of the wheel? What about you, Mate?

MATE—Captain, no man can stand up there in that sea. It would be the death of me.

CAPTAIN—It'll be the death of all of us if no one takes charge and steers us past the reefs.

HARRY—I'll go, Captain.

CAPTAIN—You!

HARRY—Yes, and I'll steer us to safety if it can be done. You've laughed at my religion, but it's meant a new way of seeing things for me. I'm prepared to die, if I have to, but I have a Master who will help me pilot this ship through the storm, just as He does my life. I'm ready, if you say so.

CAPTAIN—Harry, you're a better man than I took you for. A better man than all of us. Get up there and steer the boat, and when you come back, maybe I'll be willing to listen to what you've been trying to tell all of us.

[Curtain, and the choir sings the second stanza of the hymn. Then the READER appears.]

READER—Harry Stevens did steer the ship to safety, and, more important than that, he showed many of those on board the "Jamestown" the way to salvation. And all because he took Jesus as his Pilot. There are still storms today in the world—troublesome seas that we have to pass through. But we need not be afraid if we have the right pilot. No matter what troubles may beset us, He will steer us to the safe harbor of heaven, if we let Him be our Guide. Let us all join in singing the last stanza of "Jesus, Saviour, Pilot Me," and let us resolve to follow more closely the path He has marked out for us.

[Congregation sings last stanza.]

The Old Rugged Cross

On a hill far away, stood an old rugged cross,
   The emblem of suff'ring and shame;
And I love that old cross, where the dearest and best
   For a world of lost sinners was slain.

Chorus

So I'll cherish the old rugged cross,
   Till my trophies at last I lay down;
I will cling to the old rugged cross,
   And exchange it some day for a crown.

O that old rugged cross, so despised by the world,
   Has a wondrous attraction for me;
For the dear Lamb of God left His glory above,
   To bear it to dark Calvary.

In that old rugged cross, stained with blood so divine,
   A wondrous beauty I see;
For 'twas on that old cross Jesus suffered and died,
   To pardon and sanctify me.

To the old rugged cross I will ever be true,
   Its shame and reproach gladly bear;
Then He'll call me some day to my home far away,
   Where His glory forever I'll share.

—By George Bennard.

—Used by permission of Rodeheaver,
Hall-Mack Co., copyright owner.

The Old Rugged Cross

CHARACTERS

READER _____Preferably a young girl
WILLIAM DUSTMAN____A young man in his early twenties
MRS. DUSTMAN _____His mother, a kindly old woman
JIM BRANDT { William's friend, hardboiled, but with a kind heart

COSTUMES

Modern.

MUSIC

A choir or group of voices, offstage.

SCENE I

[*Simple room, rather bare. Suitcases in center of room.*]

READER—Few hymns have such a hold on the heart-strings of humanity as "The Old Rugged Cross." Though it is really one of our more modern hymns, it contains the old gospel message of a crucified Christ and a crown of glory for His followers. With this theme, it has sung its way into the hearts of millions. Few hymns have been of greater service in the cause of religious revivals all over the land. "The Old Rugged Cross" seems to be able to bring back memories of past allegiance to Christ, and thus it succeeds in reviving a dying or dead faith. Its author,

George Bennard, has succeeded in combining a beautiful melody with words of tremendous appeal.

Perhaps the influence of this hymn can best be observed in the life of one man, William Dustman. William is typical of thousands of young men all over our land who leave home to seek fame and fortune in the big city. Sometimes they survive the trials and temptations, but all too often, like the prodigal son, such young men only sink deeper into the mire of sin. Our story begins as William is on the point of leaving home.

[*Curtain rises, revealing* WILLIAM *and his mother putting things into a suitcase, which is almost full.*]

WILLIAM—Well, Mom, I guess we've got everything packed. That bag looks pretty full.

MRS. DUSTMAN—It won't hold much more. Oh, wait just a minute. [*Opens drawer in table and takes out book.*] I want to put your Bible in. I think it will fit in right here. [*Puts it in suitcase.*]

WILLIAM—Aw, Mom—

MRS. DUSTMAN—It won't take up much room, William. And please don't forget to read your Bible. It'll be a great comfort to you.

WILLIAM—All right, I'll take it along if it'll make you feel any better. Guess I'd better get this bag closed up. [*Struggles with it.*]

MRS. DUSTMAN [*her last effort*]—You're sure you don't want to change your mind and stay home.

WILLIAM—Now, Mom, we've been over all this before. There's nothing to keep a fellow like me in this town. I've got ideas. I want to do big things, and this is just a one-horse town.

MRS. DUSTMAN—It's not so big, William, but the people here are all nice, friendly, God-fearing folks.

WILLIAM—See—that's what I mean. The place's dead. Aw, Mom, I get tired of living right next door to the church and having to go every Sunday. I'm tired of singing hymns and listening to dry sermons. I want some life, some excitement while I'm young.

MRS. DUSTMAN—I hope you'll change your mind about some things. Maybe being in the city will make you appreciate what you had here at home. I do wish we could have gone to church tonight before you left.

WILLIAM—I wouldn't have had time to get packed and catch my train. And everybody would have had something mushy to say or a little sermon to preach to me.

MRS. DUSTMAN—Well, I won't preach to you tonight. But, listen, I think I can hear the church music. [*The choir begins to sing "The Old Rugged Cross" softly.*] The sermon must be over. Listen to that, William.

WILLIAM—I guess this is the last time I'll have to listen to church music for a long while.

MRS. DUSTMAN—They're singing "The Old Rugged Cross." [*They listen.*] That's my favorite song, William. Don't you like it, too?

WILLIAM—Yeah, it's all right, but I've got to get this suitcase out on the porch, because Sid will be here any minute now. He's going to drive me down to the station.

MRS. DUSTMAN—Well, if you must go, you must. But promise me one thing. When you're all alone in the city, take time now and then to think of your home here and those who love you. Think about hearing the choir sing "The Old Rugged Cross," and what that song means. Maybe it'll make things easier for you.

WILLIAM—You said you weren't going to preach to me.

MRS. DUSTMAN—I'm not. But promise me you'll think about those things.

WILLIAM—All right, Mom, if it'll make you feel any better. But now I've got to get going or I'll miss that train. [*Picks up suitcases.*]

CURTAIN

READER—And so William Dustman packed up and went to the big city. He thought he could leave his religion and everything fine behind him and still be a success in the world. He had big ideas and was going to do wonderful things. But, like many others, he found no place for his talents or his cynical outlook. He sank lower, sucked down by the maelstrom of the big city. He worked at any job he could get. Our next scene shows him in a cheap rooming-house, where he shares a room with an acquaintance, Jim Brandt.

SCENE II

[*A rather dirty, poverty-stricken room. Papers and clothes are strewn on the chairs and the floor. JIM is tying his tie. BILL (or WILLIAM) is sitting in a chair, reading the paper.*]

JIM—You going to look for work this morning, Bill?

WILLIAM—What's the use? I can't find anything in these want ads. Besides, it's almost noon, I guess. I pawned my watch the other day, so I can't tell what time it is except when I get hungry. But I've pounded the pavements day after day and never a nibble of a real job.

JIM—Yeah, it's kinda tough, kid. If I hadn't gotten that job as night watchman, I'd be in a bad way, too. Did you ever think of going back home? That's really what you should do.

WILLIAM—And have all the yokels laugh at me? I told them all the big things I was going to do when I came here—

and now look at me. I wouldn't dare go home now. I'd be the joke of the place.

JIM—Well, what're you going to do? You can't go on like this forever.

WILLIAM—I don't know. I met up with a couple of guys the other day who wanted me to help them stick up a bank. All I had to do was drive the car. I told them nothing doing, but maybe I'll take them up on it. I have to eat!

JIM—Don't do it, kid. Once you start that, you're gone for good. Play it the straight way. It pays in the long run.

WILLIAM—Don't preach at me. You sound like my mother.

JIM—Gee, you're a funny kid. So afraid some one will preach to you, and all the time you're wanting to go home and live like you once did.

WILLIAM—You got me all wrong, Jim.

JIM—No, I'm afraid I've got you figured out right. Oh, by the way, I forgot. The postman brought a letter for you while you were gone yesterday. [*Begins to look through pockets.*]

WILLIAM—Who was it from?

JIM—I don't know. I didn't open it. I had it here some place. Oh, here it is.

WILLIAM— [*takes letter*]—Hm. That's from my mother. [*Tosses it on chair.*]

JIM—Well, aren't you going to read it?

WILLIAM—Maybe, later. Maybe not at all. It'll be the same old things she always says.

JIM—Say, you must be crazy! There might be something wrong with her. The least you can do is read the letter.

WILLIAM—If you're so anxious to know what's in it, read it yourself.

Jim—All right, I will. It might be important. [*Opens letter and reads.*]

William [*eagerly*]—What does she say?

Jim—I thought you didn't care.

William—Well, I don't—only, so long as you're reading it—

Jim—Maybe this section might interest you. [*Reads.*] I do hope you're finding what you wanted in the city. But I'm praying that you won't forget all the things you learned here at home. I still remember how they sang "The Old Rugged Cross" the night that you went away. Do you remember that and the message in the song?

William—You don't need to read any more. I'll look at the rest myself. [*Takes letter and begins to read while* Jim *watches him closely.*]

Jim—"The Old Rugged Cross." Say, I remember that song myself. Used to sing it in Sunday school. Let me see, how did it go? [*Begins to sing the song, humming now and then when he can't remember the words. He sings to the chorus, when* William *interrupts.*]

William—Stop it! Stop singing that song. [*Grabs hold of him.*]

Jim—Why, what's the matter, Bill?

William—Nothing, nothing, only don't sing that song. You understand? I can't stand it.

Jim—You sound like you're crazy.

William—Crazy—yes, I was crazy. Crazy ever to come to this town and try to get away from God and from everything good and fine. I wanted a thrill, but all I've got is a headache out of it all.

Jim—Say, you're in a bad way. You'd better sit down in that chair and start thinking things over. [*Puts him in a chair.*]

WILLIAM—Oh, I was a fool, a fool ever to leave home! But it's too late to think about that now.

JIM—Bill, the thing for you to do is to go on home and forget about these big-city ideas.

WILLIAM—I couldn't ever face the folks back there. I bragged about all the things I was going to do. They'll laugh at me.

JIM—They laughed at the Man they nailed to the old rugged cross, too, but He didn't stop doing the right thing.

WILLIAM—I didn't know you knew anything about religion or Jesus Christ and things like that.

JIM—Maybe I haven't been thinking about them as much as I should. That song, "The Old Rugged Cross," started me doing a little wondering, too.

WILLIAM—Well, it's going to be hard, facing the folks at home. But I guess maybe I'll have the courage now. Do you suppose my mother will take me back again after I haven't written for months?

JIM—Of course she will. Mothers are like that. Her letter shows how she feels about you.

WILLIAM—Thank God you read that part to me. And thank God for "The Old Rugged Cross" that brought me to my senses.

[*Curtain, and the* READER *appears.*]

READER—And so William Dustman returned to his home and to his faith through the memories of "The Old Rugged Cross." It is hard to say just how many souls have been saved through hearing this great hymn. But as long as sin-sick souls need the message of the crucified Christ, so long will "The Old Rugged Cross" have a part to play in the work of salvation. Let us all join in singing this great revival hymn, and let us think of the Christ who died that we might some day receive a crown.

Away in a Manger

Away in a manger,
　No crib for a bed,
The little Lord Jesus
　Laid down His sweet head;
The stars in the sky
　Looked down where He lay—
The little Lord Jesus,
　Asleep on the hay.

The cattle are lowing,
　The Baby awakes,
But little Lord Jesus,
　No crying He makes;
I love Thee, Lord Jesus,
　Look down from the sky,
And stay by my cradle
　Till morning is nigh.

Be near me, Lord Jesus;
　I ask Thee to stay
Close by me forever,
　And love me, I pray.
Bless all the dear children
　In Thy tender care,
And fit us for heaven,
　To live with Thee there.
　　　　　　—Martin Luther.

Away in a Manger

CHARACTERS

MARTIN LUTHER _____ A minister
MRS. LUTHER _____His wife
JANE _____Their daughter; about eight years of age
JOHN _____Their son; nine or ten years of age
MRS. BLACK ⎫
MRS. JEFFERS ⎬ Friends of the Luther family

COSTUMES

In keeping with early sixteenth century in Germany.

SETTING

The Luther home on Christmas morning. A decorated Christmas tree with simple gifts under it.

[MR. LUTHER _is seen reading the Bible and writing as_ MRS. LUTHER _enters._]

MRS. LUTHER—Good morning, Martin. Really, I believe you will soon even quit eating so you can work. You have about quit sleeping; you have been up for hours.

MR. LUTHER—I can't sleep for thinking, so I might as well work. Don't you agree with me?

MRS. LUTHER—I suppose so, but I'm afraid all your work will not be appreciated, much less accepted.

MR. LUTHER—Maybe not, but I can't accept the doctrines that are taught in the name of Christianity.

MRS. LUTHER—To disagree is dangerous.

MR. LUTHER—I know it, but it seems to me that every Christian should be allowed the privilege of believing as he sees fit.

MRS. LUTHER—Christ was not even permitted that.

MR. LUTHER—That's true, but surely people can see that the doctrines of religion I'm writing are more like the Bible.

MRS. LUTHER—Many are afraid to see it. Not many are as brave as you.

MR. LUTHER—I couldn't do as much if it were not for you.

MRS. LUTHER—I wish I felt worthy of that compliment.

MR. LUTHER—You are worthy; you do so many things that help me. Your tolerance for what seems to be a hopeless task means so much. You make such a happy home for the children and me. Many wealthy and prominent men can not boast of as happy a home as we have.

MRS. LUTHER—That is a wife and mother's duty, whenever it is within her power.

MR. LUTHER [*smiling*]—Maybe all do not see their duty.

MRS. LUTHER—Maybe not.

MR. LUTHER—That garden you have in the summer certainly does help financially. Sometimes I wonder what we should do without it. Then you are willing to rent part of the estate, and that helps.

MRS. LUTHER—I'm only too glad to do it. When you have finished your work and study, then we can have more luxuries.

MR. LUTHER—Well, it's Christmas morning again. Seems like the years just pass on wings. The children always enjoy Christmas morning. I wish we could get them more, but we do the best we can and that's all any one can do.

MRS. LUTHER—They are always happy with what little we can get for them. The spirit of the season brings many happy hours to children, even without the gifts.

MR. LUTHER—Yes, how Jane and John do love to sing! They love the carols especially. I doubt if there is anywhere a happier home than ours at Christmas.

MRS. LUTHER—Well, we haven't as much for them as usual, but they will be happy. I hear them coming now.

[*Enter* JANE *and* JOHN *in a joyous mood.*]

JANE—Merry Christmas, Mother and Father!

JOHN—Merry Christmas!

MRS. LUTHER—And a Merry Christmas to you both, my dears. I had begun to wonder whether you had overslept, but being Christmas that seemed impossible. [*Smiles.*]

JOHN—Janie was awake a long time before I knew it. I was awake, too, but didn't hear her, and then we thought you and Father were asleep, so tried to be quiet.

[*All laugh.*]

MR. LUTHER—Very thoughtful children we have, Mother, and especially on Christmas morning.

[JANE *walks to the Christmas tree and looks longingly at the gifts.*]

MRS. LUTHER—Getting anxious?

JOHN—We always wait for Mrs. Black and Mrs. Jeffers to come over on Christmas, you know. They like to see Jane and me get our presents, and for that reason I think we should wait.

JANE—I'm willing to wait. I think they like to hear us sing, too.

[*A knock is heard at the door.* MRS. LUTHER *goes to the door, and* MRS. BLACK *and* MRS. JEFFERS *enter.*]

MRS. BLACK and MRS. JEFFERS—Merry Christmas, every one!

MR. LUTHER—Merry Christmas! And instead of saying God bless us, I'd say He has blessed us.

MRS. BLACK—How true!

[MRS. BLACK *and* MRS. JEFFERS *are seated.*]

MRS. JEFFERS—We thought you would be expecting us, so we tried to hurry.

MRS. LUTHER—We were expecting you. The children had just said that they thought you would come soon.

JOHN—Jane was getting pretty nervous.

JANE—Yes, and you were, too.

[JOHN *smiles.*]

JOHN—Do we get our presents now?

MRS. LUTHER—Yes, you may get them now. You are both old enough this year not to upset the tree, so you can get them yourselves.

JANE and JOHN—Oh, goody!

[JANE *and* JOHN *begin taking the gifts from under the tree. Each receives gifts, including their guests. At last, John picks up an envelope.*]

JOHN—Look, Jane, here is a letter for us.

[JANE *comes close to him and looks at it.*]

JANE—It's Father's writing. [*To* MR. LUTHER.] Did you play a joke on us?

MR. LUTHER—Open it and see.

[JOHN *opens it,* JANE *watching.*]

JANE—Why, it's a song!

JOHN—It surely is, but I never heard its name before.

MRS. BLACK—What is the name of your new song?

JOHN—"Away in a Manger."

MRS. JEFFERS—That must be a new one.

JANE—Look, John, it is home-printed.

MR. LUTHER—Well, children, I'll tell you about the song. Mother and I couldn't get you as much as usual this year.

You always say you like to sing the Christmas carols, so I tried writing one. I thought we could sing it together and it would be a little different.

JANE—I'm so anxious to hear it.

MRS. LUTHER—This is a surprise to me, too, but suppose we all try to sing it. It is new to us, but we can at least try.

[*All sing "Away in a Manger."*]

CURTAIN

Abide With Me

Abide with me: fast falls the eventide;
The darkness deepens; Lord, with me abide:
When other helpers fail, and comforts flee,
Help of the helpless, oh, abide with me.

Swift to its close, ebbs out life's little day;
Earth's joys grow dim, its glories pass away!
Change and decay in all around I see;
O Thou who changest not, abide with me.

Come not in terrors, as the King of kings;
But kind and good, with healing in Thy wings:
Tears for all woes, a heart for ev'ry plea;
Come, Friend of sinners, thus abide with me.

I need Thy presence every passing hour:
What but Thy grace can foil the tempter's power?
Who like Thyself my guide and stay can be?
Through cloud and sunshine, oh, abide with me.

I fear no foe, with Thee at hand to bless:
Ills have no weight, and tears no bitterness:
Where is death's sting, where, grave, thy victory?
I triumph still, if Thou abide with me!

Reveal Thyself before my closing eyes;
Shine through the gloom, and point me to the skies:
Heaven's morning breaks, and earth's vain shadows flee;
In life, in death, O Lord, abide with me!

—*Henry F. Lyte.*

Abide With Me

CHARACTERS

READER
MR. LYTE _____A kind-faced minister
THREE TOWNSMEN _____Typical business men
OLD MRS. HARRISON _____Withered and tired
JIM SAUNDERS _____A reformed drunkard

COSTUMES

Nineteenth century in England.

MUSICAL BACKGROUND

Singers do not appear during the play at all, but should be backstage. The group should be small, and it is better that they sing unaccompanied.

SCENE I

[MR. LYTE's *study*.]

READER—Some hymns have become so familiar to us that we can hardly imagine a time when they did not exist. Such a hymn is "Abide With Me," one of the best-loved songs of the Christian church. Yet, "Abide With Me" is not a hundred years old. It was written by Henry F. Lyte, of England, who served for twenty years in a rough, seafaring neighborhood. During those twenty years he had ample time to know the comfort that the abiding presence of Christ brought to his people. And so, near the end of his life he wrote "Abide With Me," almost as a story of his ministry. Since that time the hymn has cheered and strengthened Christians in many lands.

Let us imagine a few scenes in the life of Henry F. Lyte, to see where he got his message of "Abide With Me." First, he is faced with indifference among three of his church members who are also prominent business men in the community.

[*The curtain rises, revealing* MR. LYTE *and three other men seated in the room.*]

MR. LYTE—Gentlemen, I hope I can count on your support in my work here. There is much to be done.

FIRST TOWNSMAN—Well, Mr. Lyte, you understand I'm in favor of the church. But I'm a business man, and my time is valuable. I'm willing to give you all the moral support I can, but further than that I can't go.

MR. LYTE—Thank you for that, at least. [*To second townsman.*] May I count on you?

SECOND TOWNSMAN—You put me in an awkward position. Times are hard, and my business isn't any too good, either. Later on—perhaps—

MR. LYTE—I'm afraid it will be too late then. Well, there is one of you left. Surely you won't desert me. I need your help.

THIRD TOWNSMAN—I'm not a church worker, Mr. Lyte. There are too many other things that I like to do better. I'm afraid you'll have to count me out.

MR. LYTE [*getting up*]—Well, gentlemen, I suppose there is nothing more to say.

FIRST TOWNSMAN [*they all arise*]—We hope you understand, Mr. Lyte.

MR. LYTE—I think I do. Good day, gentlemen.

ALL—Good day. [*They go out.*]

Mr. Lyte—"And they straightway began to make excuse." [*Sits in chair and picks up Bible.*] It seems I am to have no help here. [*Leafs through Bible and finally reads:*] "For he hath said, I will never leave thee nor forsake thee." [*Looks up, strengthened.*] What a foolish thing—to be afraid! He will abide with me, even if others go away.

[*Curtain falls or lights dim as singers sing first stanza of "Abide With Me."*]

SCENE II

[*A plain room with two or three chairs and perhaps a cot.*]

Reader—Yes, it was hard in those days, just as it is today, to get men to serve in the kingdom. But Henry Lyte never faltered in his work. He brought comfort to souls close to death and stilled their fears with his words. Let us see him bringing peace to old Mrs. Harrison, who was about to die.

[*Scene opens with Mr. Lyte and a haggard woman seated; or she may be covered up on a small cot, if convenient.*]

Mrs. Harrison [*agitated*]—They tell me I'm going to die, Mr. Lyte. The doctors give me only three more months to live.

Mr. Lyte—I'm sorry to hear it, Mrs. Harrison, but it's something we all have to face.

Mrs. Harrison—But I'm not ready to die. I haven't lived the kind of life that I can be proud of. I just can't die.

Mr. Lyte—You can ask the forgiveness of God, Mrs. Harrison. No one can undo a lifetime in three months, but He will forgive if you ask it of Him.

Mrs. Harrison—But it's dying all alone that makes me afraid. Dying and having nobody to help you across the river.

MR. LYTE—He will take care of that, too. Listen: [*Reads from Bible.*] "Though I walk through the valley of the shadow of death, I will fear no evil; for thou art with me; thy rod and thy staff they comfort me."

MRS. HARRISON [*the light dawns*]—Thy rod and thy staff. Why—I'm not afraid any more. He'll abide with me, even to the end.

[*Curtain falls slowly and choir sings second stanza.*]

SCENE III

[*Same as Scene I.*]

READER—To every sorrowing heart comes the message of "Abide With Me." Mr. Lyte has guided many a soul through the dark waters with his song. But let us see a man touched by this humble minister. Here is one who struggled with the mighty temptations of drink—Jim Saunders.

[*Curtain opens with* SAUNDERS *and* MR. LYTE *on stage, seated.*]

SAUNDERS—I'm afraid it's no use, Mr. Lyte. I've tried to keep away from the demon rum, as you call it, but it just seems like it can't be done.

MR. LYTE—Haven't you been happier since you stayed away from that old crowd that kept you down in the mire?

SAUNDERS—Oh, yes. It's been heaven, sir, and the other was hell. But every time I pass a place where I know there's drinking going on, my legs get weak and they just seem to pull me toward that place. It's all right when some one's with me, but when I'm alone, it's just too much for me.

MR. LYTE—Ah, there's the answer to our problem. Jim, you'll have to take some one with you wherever you go.

SAUNDERS—But I can't always do that, sir. Sometimes there's nobody around to go along with me. And I can't afford to hire some one just to go around and keep me out of trouble.

MR. LYTE—You don't have to, Jim. Listen: [*Opens Bible and reads.*] "The Lord is nigh unto them that are of a broken heart; and saveth such as be of a contrite spirit. Many are the afflictions of the righteous; but the Lord delivereth him out of them all."

SAUNDERS—You mean, the Lord will be with me all the time?

MR. LYTE—Yes, Jim. You have a faithful Companion who will abide with you forever.

[*Curtain falls and singers sing third stanza.*]

READER—To those who dwell in the midst of temptations, "Abide With Me" offers a constant source of strength. There would be fewer people in the world today yielding to the snares of sin if they would remember that Jesus will abide with all who need and ask His help. But let us see one last picture in the life of Mr. Lyte. When the arduous demands of his congregation proved too much for his strength, he was forced to resign and travel in Southern Europe, where he died soon after. But before he left his congregation, he gave them one last view of his message of "Abide With Me."

SCENE IV

[*No furnishings, but an altar at one end of stage, with a cross above it. As curtain rises, MR. LYTE is standing in front of the altar as if addressing his congregation.*]

MR. LYTE—My dear Christian brethren, as you know, this is my last Sunday among you. Today I leave you, perhaps never to return. I should like nothing better than to continue to serve you, but a higher Voice than mine has spoken. My work here is through. Soon another will take my place before this altar and in your hearts. That is the way with this world, and it is right that it should be so.

And yet I leave you with the cross of Jesus Christ as a symbol of Him who changes not in His love toward all of us. Preachers and teachers may change in this church, but, if you let Him, Jesus Christ will abide with you forever. Let this cross stand as a symbol of our devotion to Him who first loved us, and may God grant that we may meet again in a happier land. God bless all of you.

[*Curtain falls slowly and last stanza of hymn is sung.*]

READER—Henry Lyte has long since left this earth, but his mighty hymn lives today in the hearts of thousands of Christians. There is no message that the Christian church needs today as much as that of the abiding presence of Jesus through all our troubles. Let us all unite in singing again this great hymn that came from a humble minister's heart and has lived to strengthen Christians everywhere.

[*Song, or a least several stanzas, by the entire group.*]

Rescue the Perishing

Rescue the perishing,
Care for the dying,
  Snatch them in pity from sin and the grave;
Weep o'er the erring one,
Lift up the fallen,
  Tell them of Jesus, the Mighty to save.

Chorus

    Rescue the perishing,
    Care for the dying;
    Jesus is merciful,
    Jesus will save.

Tho' they are slighting Him,
Still He is waiting,
  Waiting the penitent child to receive;
Plead with them earnestly,
Plead with them gently:
  He will forgive if they truly believe.

Down in the human heart,
Crushed by the tempter,
  Feelings lie buried that grace can restore;
Touched by a loving hand,
Wakened by kindness,
  Chords that were broken will vibrate once more.

Rescue the perishing,
Duty demands it;
  Strength for thy labor the Lord will provide;
Back to the narrow way
Patiently win them;
  Tell the poor wand'rer a Saviour has died.
              —*Fanny J. Crosby.*

Songs by Fanny Crosby

CHARACTERS

FANNY CROSBY _____Song writer
MRS. HAYDEN _____A friend

COMMENT

The character, Mrs. Hayden, is fictitious and used only to aid Fanny Crosby in telling her story. The person taking the part of Miss Crosby should wear dark glasses. Miss Crosby has written more than 8,000 hymns. An explanation of this to the audience is suggested.

SCENE

[*The home of* FANNY CROSBY. MISS CROSBY *is sitting with head bowed as one in a thoughtful mood. A knock is heard at the door.*]

MISS CROSBY—Come in. [MRS. HAYDEN *enters.*]

MRS. HAYDEN—Resting?

MISS CROSBY—Yes, just resting, Mrs. Hayden. Come and sit down. I'm so glad you came.

MRS. HAYDEN—You never fail to know our voices, do you?

MISS CROSBY—No, to one who can not see, I believe the sense of hearing is more discriminating. At least your voices all sound so very different to me, as different as faces look to you no doubt.

Mrs. Hayden—I was here this morning, but you were not at home.

Miss Crosby—I was gone most of the day. I had a sad though interesting trip today. I visited the slums of New York. The misery and poverty there have made me very depressed.

Mrs. Hayden—No doubt we have to visit them to understand the conditions.

Miss Crosby—How very true! I had no idea it was so bad. It is an existence, but the souls and bodies of those people are perishing.

Mrs. Hayden—You could sense the conditions which you could not see?

Miss Crosby—Indeed I could. Eyesight couldn't have made me any more conscious of the plight of these poor people. The children are so pathetic, also the elderly people and even those in the prime of life. I doubt if there is any prime of life for them, however.

Mrs. Hayden—Crime and unbelief stalk hand in hand with starvation.

Miss Crosby—Yes, if only the story of a loving Saviour could be told them! It would change their lives.

Mrs. Hayden—You frequently hear the statement that they wouldn't live any better if they could. Do you believe that?

Miss Crosby—These people have lived in this condition for so many generations it would take time to teach them. It could be done if we would try; it might be a long, tedious task, but I know it could be accomplished at least in part. It would take gentle treatment, pleading and love. Those people have broken spirits, their feelings are hardened. With patience and understanding we would discover buried in their hearts feelings the same as ours.

MRS. HAYDEN—There are organizations and churches carrying on this work, don't you think?

MISS CROSBY—Yes, there are, but not enough, I hope I can in some way get people to see how much they need our help. I have been planning and thinking ever since I came home on what I could do to help in this cause. The conditions should be brought to the attention of the public in a more forceful way.

MRS. HAYDEN—Have you arrived at any decision or formulated any plan?

MISS CROSBY [*smiling*]—No, I haven't. So far, I have done only one thing; I have written a song about it.

MRS. HAYDEN—A song?

MISS CROSBY—Yes, it is a plea to help these unfortunate people. It may reach more people that way. It seems I can always express myself better in verse than in any other way. I have tried to picture these people in the New York slums and then make a plea for their help.

MRS. HAYDEN—How very interesting! May I see the poem?

MISS CROSBY—It is there on the table, I think. Read it and see if you think I have made a plea for these unfortunates.

[MRS. HAYDEN *takes paper and begins to read. Singers offstage sing "Rescue the Perishing."*]

MRS. HAYDEN—That is certainly a picture of the people and a plea for help for them. Does it take you long to write these poems which usually are set to music?

MISS CROSBY—As a rule, it takes me a very short time. Sometimes I compose them as rapidly as I can dictate; others take longer.

MRS. HAYDEN—To be able to do that is truly a gift. How long have you been writing?

Miss Crosby—I was writing some at the age of eight, but I wrote almost constantly after I was fifteen. You knew, however, that at first I didn't write poems suitable to become hymns?

Mrs. Hayden—No, I didn't. I supposed all of your writings had been of a religious nature.

Miss Crosby—My first writings were not religious. I began to write poems for hymns after I was forty-four. It was Mr. Bradbury, the composer, who started me to writing hymns. I have always felt a debt of gratitude to him, for I have been so much happier. My life has meant so much more, and I feel I have made a much better contribution to the world.

Mrs. Hayden—Did you have any particular reason for writing "Safe in the Arms of Jesus"?

Miss Crosby—No, I had never thought about it until one day when W. H. Doane came to see me. You know, he has written tunes for so many hymns. This particular day, Mr. Doane came and told me he had a new tune. He played it for me and the words of "Safe in the Arms of Jesus" seemed to sing themselves to me as he played. When he finished, I went to another room and wrote the words.

Mrs. Hayden—Do you mean to tell me that you could remember the words long enough to write all of them down? I should have thought that, even if they came to you as he played, you would have forgotten them by the time he had finished. The theme might have remained in my memory, but not the whole poem.

Miss Crosby—Well, it did!

Mrs. Hayden—You wrote "All the Way My Saviour Leads Me," too, I believe.

Miss Crosby—Yes, I did, but it had no story like "Rescue the Perishing" to prompt its writing. However, knowing how much I must depend on others in many respects, you can see why I wrote it. I have learned in my blindness to rely on the Saviour, and He has led me all the way. I was only six weeks old when I became blind through accident. I determined never to lament my plight, and when I felt my dependence I leaned on Jesus. My ambition since writing hymns has been to help win those who know not Christ.

MRS. HAYDEN—I am so happy to have learned more about you and your writings.

["*Safe in the Arms of Jesus*" and "*All the Way My Saviour Leads Me*" are sung offstage.]

CURTAIN

I Would Be True

I would be true, for there are those who trust me;
I would be pure, for there are those who care;
I would be strong, for there is much to suffer;
I would be brave, for there is much to dare,
I would be brave, for there is much to dare.

I would be friend of all—the foe, the friendless;
I would be giving, and forget the gift;
I would be humble, for I know my weakness;
I would look up and laugh and love and lift,
I would look up and laugh and love and lift.

—Howard Arnold Walter.

I Would Be True

CHARACTERS

HOWARD WALTER _____A young college student
JOHN PAYNE _____Howard's roommate
MRS. WALTER _____Howard's mother
MRS. PRESTON _____A friend of the Walter family
MRS. DUNCAN _____Another friend

COSTUMES

Period of 1906 to 1918.

SCENE I

[*A room in Waseda College dormitory in Japan.* HOWARD *is seated at a table studying as* JOHN *enters.*]

JOHN—Hello, there, old pal, not working hard, are you? [*Throws books on the table and drops into a chair at the table.*]

HOWARD—Yes, I really have been working pretty hard, but I don't think hard work ever hurt very many of us. [*Smiles.*]

JOHN—Well, my last exam is over and *am I glad!* Really, Howard, do you enjoy life in old Japan as much as you did at Princeton?

HOWARD—Oh, I suppose it isn't as pleasant as our four years at Princeton, but think of our future. We must take the bitter with the sweet if we ever get any place in this world.

121

JOHN—I know that, too, but . . .

HOWARD—But life didn't seem so interesting at Princeton, either, until we were away from it. Now did it? Funny creatures, aren't we?

JOHN—That old saying that home is always best is true; but we don't realize it while there.

HOWARD—That's true, but life is like that; we never appreciate the value of things in the present. Nevertheless, we have dedicated our lives to Christ and should not have time to be pessimistic.

JOHN—I almost envy you your disposition; you always find a reason to be happy.

HOWARD—Not always, perhaps, but I have one motive in life—I would be true to my Christ and all mankind. This should keep me so busy that I'll have no time to be depressed.

JOHN—Howard, I'm no flatterer, but your influence on my life has been immeasurable. They say the good die young, and sometimes I wonder why you are still living.

HOWARD—Quit your kidding; we were really talking seriously, I thought.

JOHN—I am serious.

HOWARD—Let's change the subject. When you came in, I wasn't in a very happy frame of mind, I'm afraid.

JOHN—No? That's very strange to hear you say that.

HOWARD—May be strange, but it's true just the same.

JOHN—What's the matter, no letter from your girl?

HOWARD—[*Smiles.*] Talk about me being easily made happy. A girl can make you forget you ever had a trouble or care in the world.

JOHN—Who wouldn't appreciate seeing an American girl? In another six months I'll even forget what one looks like.

HOWARD—Cheer up. We shall be going home one of these days.

JOHN [*thoughts seem far away*]— Home! And it's near Christmas.

HOWARD—That's what I meant when I said I was a little depressed. The Christmas season is near, and I can't seem to catch the spirit in this strange land. One naturally thinks of home at Christmas.

JOHN—We never get too old to want to be at home on Christmas.

HOWARD—The thought of Mother alone in the States is not a happy one. If I could only remember her with a small gift, but finances won't permit that. You know, John, I've got a *real* mother.

JOHN—I'll say you have! Your mother has been a real pal to you; she is always so helpful, too. There is one outstanding characteristic she has that has meant so much to me; she makes you feel she has confidence in you at all times. Always seems to understand—even when we were just children, she did.

HOWARD—Then you wonder why I say that my motive in life is to remain true to the principles of Christ. I have given my life to Him, and Mother has confidence that when the testing times come I'll remain true.

JOHN—I've rather avoided the thought of Christmas for the same reason. I have no money to spend for Christmas, but there is no use to worry about it. There is nothing I can do.

HOWARD—Well, I've done the best I could about it. I have written a little poem and am sending it to Mother. That will have to be her Christmas gift this year. [*Smiles.*]

JOHN—You always did like to write poetry, didn't you? You were getting rather good at it before you came here.

HOWARD—I have named it "My Creed." Maybe it will reassure her that I am still remaining true to my convictions—but she never doubts me anyway. The words kept running through my mind, so I decided to write it and send it to her. I am more determined to lead a Christian life than ever before since I see the dire need on every hand in these countries.

JOHN—I'll bet your mother will prize that more than any present you could send her. Who knows, some day you may be a famous writer.

HOWARD—You certainly are lavish in your flattery today. There isn't anything you want, is there? [*Smiles.*]

JOHN—There you go again accusing me of flattery. I mean every word I've said. You wouldn't be the first person to gain fame through a hobby, would you? Who knows, your writings may be your greatest contribution to humanity!

HOWARD—I wish I were worthy of your remarks, but I am not. Nevertheless, I appreciate your friendship and esteem. I hope I shall always be worthy of it. We are both in a rather serious mood for young men, don't you think?

JOHN—Seems that way. Well, I feel in better spirits, anyway, just having this little chat, even if it has been rather rambling. Guess I'll write the folks a letter. It should reach there by Christmas; I can do no more, so I'll have to let it go at that.

HOWARD—That is a wise idea. When we have done our best we can do no more. We neither one have money to buy gifts so we will do the next best thing and forget it. I have written Mother this poem, and it is all I can do, but I have so much to be thankful for, so why worry?

[HOWARD *seals his letter and begins to read.* JOHN *is writing his letter.*]

CURTAIN

124

SCENE II

[*The* WALTER *home, five years later.* MRS. WALTER *sits with bowed head.* HOWARD *enters.*]

HOWARD—Well, Mother, I am all packed and ready to go. I didn't think it would be such a task. If you hadn't helped me, no telling when I would have finished. Just think, Mother, at last I am ready to start to do something worth while. At least I hope I can accomplish enough to feel that I am doing a little good anyway.

MRS. WALTER—Of course you will do a great many things that will be worth while; in fact, you have even now.

HOWARD—I'm afraid you are wrong there. I have so far been on the receiving end of life and contributed nothing.

MRS. WALTER—No, Howard, that is not true. You have given me more pleasure now than the average son does his mother.

HOWARD—You naturally would think that, but I am no sissy and have done many things I should not have done.

MRS. WALTER—Indeed you are no sissy, for that type of person doesn't have the stamina to remain true in the face of many obstacles.

HOWARD—Mother, you are a great inspiration. I hope I shall always live up to your expectations. I would sooner have it said that I remained true to my Christian convictions than anything I know. Our lives are lessons to others.

MRS. WALTER—How true that is, Son!

HOWARD—The time is getting short, and let's not make this parting a sad one. Who knows what may happen before we are together again? [*Assumes a cheerful attitude.*] I shall be a settled businesslike Y. M. C. A. secretary the next time you see me; I may even have a few gray hairs. [*Both laugh.*]

MRS. WALTER—You are the same optimistic son that you were when a small boy—always looking on the optimistic side of life.

HOWARD—[*Walks to window and looks out.*] Well, there is one thing that won't be so humorous and that is if I miss my train, which also means I would miss the boat.

MRS. WALTER—John is taking you to the train, isn't he?

HOWARD—Yes, but I thought he would be here by now. Faithful old John. How I shall miss him! How I wish he had decided to go to India, too, but maybe he can do more good here.

MRS. WALTER—This will be the first time you and John have been separated long for a number of years.

HOWARD—Yes, we were boys together. Then followed our years in Princeton, then Waseda College, in Japan, and the past year, even though he was not in the Seminary, I saw him often. [*Looks toward the window again.*] There he comes now. [JOHN *enters.*]

HOWARD—I had begun to think you had forgotten me.

JOHN—Oh, no, I'd never do that, much as I would like to in this case; then maybe you would stay at home. [*Looks toward* MRS. WALTER.] How do you do, Mrs. Walter, can't you persuade this boy to stay at home where he belongs?

MRS. WALTER—I shall miss him, too, but Howard feels very definitely he is needed in India. Since this is true, I am happy to see him start out to do the thing he has worked so hard to prepare himself to do.

JOHN—Yes, I know you are right, but I shall be lost without him. I'll tell you, I'll be your son while he is away. You need a son and I need a mother. What do you say? [*All laugh.*]

MRS. WALTER—That's a bargain.

HOWARD—You be sure you make her a good son.

JOHN—Oh, I'll do that all right. Well, where is the baggage? We must be starting. [*Picks up Gladstone bag and leaves.*]

HOWARD—Same old John. First he is up on the mountain tops, then he is down in the valley.

MRS. WALTER—John is a great boy. Now, Son, be careful of your health, and do write often. I shall be very lonely at times. India is so far away and the dangers so great. Remember the Great Commission and keep ever true. It is needless to remind you to do that, however, for I know you will.

HOWARD—I shall try to do that. Now, please, Mother, let us make this parting as happy as we can even though our hearts are sad. Just think how happy we shall be when I return. Come to the door with me and tell me good-by as you always did when I left for college. [*They walk to the door together.* HOWARD *takes her hand in his.*] Good-by, Mother, I'll write often.

MRS. WALTER—Good-by, Son, may God bless you and keep you. [HOWARD *leaves and* MRS. WALTER *stands with bowed head. Then faces the audience with eyes uplifted. Prays.*] Dear God, protect my boy, and if it be Thy will, bring him back to me; if it be not Thy will, keep him ever true and may he never fail to serve Thee. He is so brave, so true and loyal. Give me courage to face the coming days. Amen.

CURTAIN

SCENE III

[MRS. PRESTON'S *home.* MRS. PRESTON *is reading the paper, when a knock is heard at the door. She goes to the door and opens it.* MRS. DUNCAN *enters.*]

Mrs. Preston—Good morning, Mrs. Duncan. How are you?

Mrs. Duncan—I'm feeling much better, thank you. I shouldn't take the time to stop, but I was on my way to the store and couldn't resist stopping a few minutes.

Mrs. Preston—I'm glad you did stop. We are all in such a hurry we seldom take time to appreciate each other; then the first thing you know one of our friends is taken and we are sorry we were in such a hurry.

Mrs. Duncan—That is undoubtedly true.

Mrs. Preston—It would seem that this year with all its sorrow should teach us a lesson. I've wished so many times since the death of many of our friends that I had taken more time to cultivate their friendship.

Mrs. Duncan—I've thought of that so many times. The most nerve-racking moments of the war have been this year, and 1918 has certainly been a year of sickness and death.

Mrs. Preston—This flu epidemic has been almost beyond endurance. With so much suffering and sorrow I wonder why more people haven't lost their minds.

Mrs. Duncan—Just think of Mrs. Walter—and, of course, there are hundreds more who are enduring the same sorrow.

Mrs. Preston—She certainly is a brave woman, though.

Mrs. Duncan—I marvel at her courage. I've thought of her so much since Howard's death. She was so devoted to him, and had built up such high hopes in his success and then to have him taken so early in life.

Mrs. Preston [picks up paper which is lying in her lap and glances at it]—I was just reading an article about him in this paper when you came in. Oh, here it is. Hartford Seminary has placed his name on the honor roll.

Mrs. Duncan—Is that so? That may be some comfort to her to know that his good work is still being remembered. It just doesn't seem right that he should have been taken.

Mrs. Preston—I know it doesn't seem right. It is not our place to question the works of the Lord, but we are all so human that at least we wonder. On the other hand, we do not know what great good has been accomplished, even in his short life.

Mrs. Duncan—He was a wonderful boy in every respect. I understand John Payne, his pal, is almost frantic. You know they were such close friends all during their school days.

Mrs. Preston—I don't doubt that. Mrs. Walter said that John had been such a comfort to her since Howard's death.

Mrs. Duncan—Howard wasn't sick long, was he?

Mrs. Preston—He was sick several weeks, but never gave up. There were so many sick that he kept going and had no resistance when he finally did have to give up. The flu has been so bad over there, too. Did you ever hear that he had written several poems for publication?

Mrs. Duncan—Yes, I have heard something about it, but nothing definite. I do know that he did have quite a lot of poetic ability.

[A knock is heard at the door.]

Mrs. Preston—Excuse me, please. [Goes to the door, opens it, and Mrs. Walter enters.]

Mrs. Walter—Good morning. Are you too busy for callers? [Smiles.]

Mrs. Preston—No, indeed. Come right in. Mrs. Duncan and I were just chatting a bit. Have a chair.

Mrs. Walter—Good morning, Mrs. Duncan, are you feeling better? [Seats herself.]

Mrs. Duncan—Much better, thank you. I had the "flu" only a few days, for which I am very thankful.

Mrs. Walter—You should be. My, these times are terrible.

Mrs. Preston—Mrs. Duncan and I were just reading about Howard's name being placed on the honor roll at Hartford Seminary. It must be a great consolation to you to know that Howard was so respected by all who knew him.

Mrs. Walter—Indeed it has been. His passing seemed more than I could bear, at first, but I have tried to be brave, for that is the way Howard would want me to be. The hardest thing to bear was the fact that I could not see him in his illness. In fact, he was gone before I knew anything about it.

Mrs. Duncan—The Y. M. C. A. officials wrote you the details, didn't they?

Mrs. Walter—[Wipes eyes with her handkerchief hurriedly so as not to be noticed.] Yes, I have had some of the loveliest letters from them telling how brave he was. If he had given up sooner he probably would have recovered, but that was never Howard's way. He had so much determination.

Mrs. Preston—I hope you will not think me rude for being so inquisitive, but Mrs. Duncan and I were just saying when you came in that we had heard that Howard had written poems for publication and we wondered if it were true.

Mrs. Walter—It is true that he did write several poems, but he had never intended them for publication. He was very fond of poetry, and had considerable talent in writing it.

Mrs. Preston—I have heard you say that before, I think.

Mrs. Walter—You remember when Howard was in Waseda University in Japan, in 1906, don't you?

Mrs. Preston—Oh, yes.

Mrs. Walter—Well, that Christmas, Howard felt that he had nothing to send me for a gift, so he wrote a short poem and sent it to me saying that it would have to serve as my Christmas present for that year. He was a little downhearted when he wrote it, so John Payne told me later. This was rather unusual for Howard. In this poem he was endeavoring to put into words his life's creed. In fact, he named it "My Creed."

Mrs. Duncan—I have read a few of his poems and they were very good.

Mrs. Walter—Now to finish my story. I thought this poem was very well written, so without telling Howard, I sent it to "Harper's Magazine." They published it, but changed the name to "I Would Be True" and now it has been set to music. I had planned on surprising Howard with it when he came home, but that was never to be. Now that it has been set to music I am so happy.

Mrs. Preston—Isn't that wonderful? I am glad, too.

Mrs. Duncan—I am sure you are consoled in your loss by knowing that Howard's gift to the world shall live on.

Mrs. Preston—Doesn't that prove what we were saying, Mrs. Duncan? We were just saying that we never know what influence even those who die young may have.

Mrs. Walter—This has reconciled me to my loss more than anything. I hope this may be the means of leading many other young people to take the words of this song as their creed. Yes, the year 1918 took from me a son, but the year 1906 gave to the world a song.

["*I Would Be True*" is sung offstage.]

[CURTAIN]

America the Beautiful

O beautiful for spacious skies,
   For amber waves of grain,
For purple mountain majesties
   Above the the fruited plain!
America!   America!
   God shed His grace on thee,
And crown thy good with brotherhood,
   From sea to shining sea!

O beautiful for pilgrim feet,
   Whose stern, impassioned stress
A thoroughfare for freedom beat
   Across the wilderness!
America!   America!
   God mend thine ev'ry flaw,
Confirm thy soul in self-control,
   Thy liberty in law!

O beautiful for heroes proved
   In liberating strife,
Who more than self their country loved,
   And mercy more than life!
America!   America!
   May God thy gold refine
Till all success be nobleness
   And ev'ry gain divine!

O beautiful for patriot dream
   That sees beyond the years
Thine alabaster cities gleam,
   Undimmed by human tears!
America!   America!
   God shed His grace on thee,
And crown thy good with brotherhood,
   From sea to shining sea!

—*Katherine Lee Bates.*

America the Beautiful

CHARACTERS

KATHERINE LEE BATES { Professor of English at Wellesley College

JANET WILSON _____ A student at Wellesley

COSTUMES

Late nineteenth century.

SUGGESTION

In order to have Miss Bates tell her own story of the writing of this hymn, the fictitious character, Janet Wilson, has been used. An explanation to the audience to this effect is suggested.

[MISS BATES'S *study. Time, about 1900.* MISS BATES *is seated at her desk, reading. A knock is heard at the door.*]

MISS BATES—Come in.

[JANET *enters; has songbook in her hand.* MISS BATES *rises as she enters.*]

JANET—Are you very busy, Miss Bates?

MISS BATES—Not especially. Glad to see you. Sit down.

[MISS BATES *resumes her seat at her desk.* JANET *sits opposite her.*]

JANET [*hesitatingly*]—My reason for coming, Miss Bates, is not in regard to my English work in your classes. Would you rather I came some other time?

133

Miss Bates—Oh, no. I shall be glad to talk with you.

Janet—If you only knew how all the students admire you because you are always willing to give us so much of your time!

Miss Bates—Janet, I have always thought that that was a teacher's duty—to talk with students whenever possible. I believe that is especially true of teachers in colleges. So you see I am doing my duty and I enjoy the contact with my students—perhaps more than they do.

Janet—I'm sure they enjoy it and derive much good from it.

Miss Bates—You say your visit is not prompted because you need help with your English. Then it must be homesickness. [*Smiles.*]

Janet—Neither one. Miss Bates, I have always loved the song, "America the Beautiful." Since coming to Wellesley College I have learned that you are the one who wrote it.

Miss Bates—If you refer to the words, you are correct. I did write the words, but not the music.

Janet—Well, you see, I have appreciated so many of our songs more after I learned why they were written. I have found that a great many inspiring incidents prompted the writing of many of our songs.

Miss Bates—I agree with you. The true beauty is lost in many songs because we do not know why the author wrote them. Being a teacher of English, I naturally am interested in the facts surrounding any writing.

Janet—That is the reason I came today, Miss Bates. I should like to know how you happened to write "America the Beautiful."

Miss Bates [*smiles*]—I see. Well, first let me ask you several questions. Did you ever think of that song as a journey?

134

JANET [*thoughtfully*]—No, I didn't.

MISS BATES—As you read or sang the words you thought just of the word "America" in general?

JANET [*slowly*]—I probably did.

MISS BATES [*smiling*]—You never visualized Colorado Springs or Pikes Peak, did you?

JANET—Why no, I didn't.

MISS BATES—I am finding this interesting myself. I realize, as never before, how much we lose when we fail to find out the background of any writing. Now for the story. In 1893, I was invited to teach at a summer school in Colorado Springs. You realize that the journey from Wellesley College to Colorado Springs gave me the opportunity of practically crossing the United States. I never enjoyed anything so much as that trip. Nature was at her loveliest. Do you have the song there in that book?

JANET [*opening book*]—Yes, I do.

MISS BATES—I believe you will follow me better if you follow the song while I explain. One day, soon after arriving at Colorado Springs, I made a trip to Pikes Peak. Words can not picture how beautiful it all was; I tried, however. The opening lines came to me as I stood on Pikes Peak, where I could gaze off into the distance. I could see for miles, it seemed, and I thought of the spacious skies. And so it was there I thought of the lines I wrote about the skies and the mountains. You know a mountain always seems purple in the distance. Upon returning to my room in Colorado Springs, my mind still lingered on the beauty of Pikes Peak. As I sat alone with my thoughts, I jotted down those two lines. Then I thought of other scenes which had impressed me vividly on my trip West.

JANET—The plains you spoke of as fruited were in the Middle West, I imagine.

Miss Bates—Exactly. I remembered how colorful those vast fields of grain were and I fitted them into my first two lines. By this time I was so interested I decided to try at least to make a word picture of that trip. I began, as I wrote, to realize how grateful we should be to those who dared to venture into the West many years ago. From this thought came the lines about the pilgrims or pioneers. They were truly lovers of freedom—and such courageous people! I thought of all the beauties of nature we should have missed had the West never been settled. Now can you guess where I saw the alabaster cities?

Janet—I was just wondering about that, but I'm afraid I could not even venture a guess.

Miss Bates [*smiling*]—On my way to Colorado Springs, I stopped in Chicago several days. The Columbian Exposition was then in progress, and the buildings were white and so beautiful. They resembled alabaster, and were so numerous they resembled a city. As all expositions do, the future was depicted, and I thought of these new things to come as a patriot's dream. Feeling very deeply how much we should love America and what a beautiful country it was, I decided to end each verse with a prayer. Surely, we ought always to pray for the safety of so beautiful a land. That, Janet, is how I came to write the words.

Janet—How can I ever thank you for taking the time to tell me all this? I shall love the song more than ever now, and I shall always think of it as your trip from the East to the West.

[Miss Bates *and* Janet *sing the song. If those taking these parts are unable to sing, a quartet or duet may be used.*]

CURTAIN

God Will Take Care of You

Be not dismayed whate'er betide,
  God will take care of you;
Beneath His wings of love abide,
  God will take care of you.

Chorus

God will take care of you
  Thro' every day
  O'er all the way
He will take care of you;
God will take care of you.

Thro' days of toil, when heart doth fail,
  God will take care of you;
When dangers fierce your path assail,
  God will take care of you.

All you may need He will provide,
  God will take care of you;
Nothing you ask will be denied,
  God will take care of you.

No matter what may be the test,
  God will take care of you;
Lean, weary one, upon His breast,
  God will take care of you.

                —*By C. D. Martin.*

—Used by permission of Hope Publishing Co., copyright owner.

God Will Take Care of You

CHARACTERS

READER _____A young girl
W. S. MARTIN _____A minister in his early forties
MRS. MARTIN _____His wife, who has been ill
"A. G." MARTIN _____The young son

COSTUMES

Of about 1905.

MUSIC

A choir or group of voices. These should not appear on stage, although they do not have to be concealed.

SCENE I

[*A simple room.*]

READER—In this modern world of ours, sometimes even the bravest Christian grows afraid. The forces of evil seem too strong. Temptations loom on every side. Against all this, the Christian feels helpless and beaten. But in the midst of these moments of fear, every believer can find strength and reassurance in the great hymn, "God Will Take Care of You." The song contains a message for the weak and fainthearted. The Christian is reminded that he lives under the protecting hand of God. Regardless of the strength of the powers of evil, God is with those who love Him. Every true believer should feel better prepared to meet life's battles after he has sung this great hymn.

Few people know the story behind "God Will Take Care of You." It represents the result of a trial of faith in the lives of its authors. Mrs. C. D. Martin wrote the words of the hymn, and her husband, W. S. Martin, supplied the music. The idea was suggested by their small son. But let us see how this well-beloved song of Christian comfort came to be written.

[*The curtain rises, showing* Mrs. Martin *half reclining in a bed. She is ill.* Mr. Martin *and* "A. G." *are also in the room, both very anxious about the sick woman.*]

Mr. Martin—Now, dear, please don't spare our feelings any more. Tell me truthfully, how do you feel? Are you any better?

Mrs. Martin—I'm afraid I'm sicker than I thought. My head still feels giddy and it hurts so when I have to cough.

Mr. Martin—You shouldn't be sitting up like this. You ought to lie down.

Mrs. Martin—No, I'm all right. I can breathe much better when I'm sitting up.

"A. G."—[*Running to Mrs. Martin.*] Aren't you well yet, Mamma?

Mrs. Martin—Not quite. How's Mamma's big boy?

"A. G."—Oh, I'm all right. But I wish you'd hurry and get well so we can play together and go for walks like we usually do.

Mr. Martin—You mustn't worry your mother, Son. She's ill.

"A. G."—Aren't you going to church to preach, Daddy?

Mr. Martin—I don't know whether to go or not. If I'd realized how sick Mother was going to be, I'd have gotten some one to take my place. But it's too late for that now.

MRS. MARTIN—You must go and keep your appointment to preach, Walter. What will the people think if there's no service?

MR. MARTIN—I know. I hate to disappoint them.

MRS. MARTIN—Of course you must go. Suppose some one who's never heard the message of the gospel should be there. He might perish without your words of comfort.

MR. MARTIN—I have a sermon today especially prepared for such a person.

MRS. MARTIN—Then you must go and preach. I'll be all right here.

MR. MARTIN—But I can't bear to leave you here suffering like this. It would be difficult for me to preach any kind of a sermon. I'd be thinking of you all the time.

[MRS. MARTIN *has a violent coughing spell.*]

"A. G."—Mamma, it sounds like it hurts.

MRS. MARTIN—It does, dear—a little.

MR. MARTIN [*putting hat down*]—That settles it. They'll just have to do without preaching today. I'm going to stay home, my dear, and take care of you.

"A. G."—But Daddy, if God wants you to preach today, won't He take care of Mamma while you're gone?

MRS. MARTIN—There's the answer to your problem, dear. "A. G." is right. I'll be perfectly safe here in God's care.

MR. MARTIN—I guess I had forgotten that. Sometimes a little child does lead us to a great truth. You're in safer hands than mine, so I guess it's all right for me to go.

MRS. MARTIN—Yes, Walter. We've nothing to fear as long as we trust in Him.

MR. MARTIN [*gathering up books and papers*]—Well, I'll have to hurry if I'm going to get there on time. I hope you will be much better when I get back.

MRS. MARTIN—I'm sure I shall be. The thought that God takes care of me has already made me feel stronger. [MR. MARTIN *pats her on the shoulder.*] Good-by, and God be with you in your sermon.

"A. G."—Good-by, Daddy.

[*Curtain, and the hymn is hummed by choir as* READER *reads the next section.*]

READER—And so Mr. Martin went to keep his preaching appointment, encouraged by the remark of his small son. But that statement did even more. It strengthened Mrs. Martin with its assurance of God's protection and set her mind to work. Her husband was due for a surprise when he returned.

SCENE II

[*Same as Scene I.* MRS. MARTIN *is propped up in bed as before, but there are several sheets of paper with writing on them strewn on the floor and bed. She holds one piece in her hand and is reading it to herself. "A. G." wanders toward the door or window.*]

"A. G."—Oh, Mamma, here comes Daddy. Church must be over already.

MRS. MARTIN—I'm so glad he went to the services. Every one would have been so disappointed to come to church and find the preacher not there.

[MR. MARTIN *enters.* "A. G." *runs over to him.*]

"A. G."—Daddy, Daddy.

MR. MARTIN—Hello, Son. Hello, dear. How are you feeling now?

MRS. MARTIN—I'm so much better. I've really gotten stronger every minute.

MR. MARTIN—That's fine. But I knew you would. I just trusted that God was taking care of you.

MRS. MARTIN—How was the service? Did you have a good crowd?

MR. MARTIN—Excellent, my dear. It would have been too bad if I hadn't gone. The words of my sermon struck home to three unsaved souls, and they told me afterwards that they were willing to give their hearts to Christ.

MRS. MARTIN—And they might never have been won if you hadn't gone.

MR. MARTIN—That's true. I guess "A. G." has taught us a lesson. We must be more trusting and not neglect our duties.

MRS. MARTIN—That's right. Now I've got a surprise for you. I've been busy while you were gone.

MR. MARTIN—Now, you haven't been stirring around and working, have you? You're not strong enough for that.

MRS. MARTIN—No, dear, nothing like that. But I've been writing some poetry. Just a few verses.

MR. MARTIN—Oh, good! Let me see it.

MRS. MARTIN [hands paper to husband]—It's meant to be a hymn. Perhaps you can compose a tune for it.

MR. MARTIN—Let me see. [Reads first stanza and chorus.]

> Be not dismayed whate'er betide,
>   God will take care of you;
> Beneath His wings of love abide,
>   God will take care of you.

> God will take care of you,
>   Thro' every day,
>   O'er all the way;
> He will take care of you,
> God will take care of you.

Why, dear, that's fine!

MRS. MARTIN—The last lines are meant to serve as a chorus.

MR. MARTIN [*begins to hum to himself*]—How's this for the first line? [*Sings it through.*] Now for the next. How's this? [*Sings through second line, hesitatingly.*]

MRS. MARTIN —I believe you've got a start. Couldn't you just repeat that for the next two lines?

MR. MARTIN—Yes, that would go all right. Then this can be the tune for the verse. [*Sings it all through to the chorus.*]

MRS. MARTIN—I like that. But you must get a good chorus to go with it.

MR. MARTIN—That's right. Let me see. [*Tries several tunes without success.*] This is harder. I can't seem to get any ideas.

MRS. MARTIN—Oh, you must, you must! You're off to such a good start.

MR. MARTIN—Well, I'll try again. [*Reads words of chorus. Tries several notes.*] Now! Now it's coming to me. [*Feels way through chorus.*] That's it! Listen. [*Sings chorus through again.*] Do you like it?

MRS. MARTIN—Oh, yes! The music seems to fit with the words so well. Hurry and write it down before you forget it.

MR. MARTIN—All right, I'll go play it and write the music in just a moment. But let's sing it together once so I'll know that you really do feel better.

MRS. MARTIN—All right, dear. [*They start to sing as the curtain falls. The choir takes it up and finishes the stanza.*]

READER—And so the great hymn was written. It represented a real experience to Mr. and Mrs. Martin, a lesson that they never forgot. Perhaps that is why the hymn has always been a favorite of Christians everywhere. It comes so close to our own lives. As long as trials and troubles beset us, this hymn will probably retain its popularity, for it brings us the message of Him who said, "Come unto me, all ye that labor and are heavy laden, and I will give you rest." The song strengthens us and helps us continue our tasks in this world. Let us all unite in singing the hymn and in thinking of its glorious message.

In the Garden

I come to the garden alone,
    While the dew is still on the roses;
And the voice I hear,
Falling on my ear,
    The Son of God discloses.

Chorus

And He walks with me, and He talks with me,
    And He tells me I am His own;
And the joy we share as we tarry there,
    None other has ever known.

He speaks, and the sound of His voice
    Is so sweet the birds hush their singing;
And the melody
That He gave to me,
    Within my heart is ringing.

I'd stay in the garden with Him,
    Tho' the night around me be falling;
But He bids me go:
Thro' the voice of woe,
    His voice to me is calling.

—*By C. Austin Miles.*

—Used by permission of Rodeheaver,
    Hall-Mack Co., copyright owner.

In the Garden

CHARACTERS

JOHN ROBBINS ....A boy about eight years of age
MRS. ROBBINS ....His mother

COSTUMES

Modern.

SCENE I

[*The* ROBBINS *home.* MRS. ROBBINS *is reading a book as* JOHN *enters.*]

JOHN—Hello there, Mother.

MRS. ROBBINS—I was just thinking it was about time for you to come in.

[JOHN *seats himself on a stool close to his mother.*]

JOHN—It was getting dark and we couldn't see to play ball any more.

MRS. ROBBINS—Do you have all your lessons for to-morrow?

JOHN—Didn't have any assigned for tonight. That's a break, don't you think?

MRS. ROBBINS—I suppose. [*Smiles.*]

JOHN—What are you reading?

MRS. ROBBINS—A book about hymns.

JOHN [*with a puzzled attitude*]—Hymns? What is there to read about them? You mean you are reading

147

hymns? [*Gets up and looks over* MRS. ROBBINS' *shoulder.*] But that's not a hymnbook.

MRS. ROBBINS—No, it's not a hymnbook. [*John sits down on the stool again. Looks up at his mother.*] It is stories about hymns and about their writers. Some very interesting stories are connected with their writing.

JOHN—I always imagined the writers just thought of a name for a song and then wrote the words. Or thought of some lines of poetry they liked and named them. You know, like our teacher does sometimes. She gives us a subject and then says to write something about it.

MRS. ROBBINS—No, John, very few of our hymns were written that way. The composer usually had a purpose. Some of them, in fact, a number of them, were inspired by sorrow.

JOHN—How could that be? I can't write anything if I'm sad.

MRS. ROBBINS—You will think differently as you grow older. However, some of them were written because of happiness in the composer's life. It seems that there are some who could forget their sadness by writing. I've discovered that if we know what the writer had in mind when he or she wrote the song it means more.

JOHN—Our teacher told us how Francis Scott Key came to write "The Star Spangled Banner."

MRS. ROBBINS—Didn't you enjoy the song more then?

JOHN—Sure!

MRS. ROBBINS—Well, the same is true of all songs.

JOHN—Would you tell me one of the stories now?

MRS. ROBBINS—I'll be glad to. What song would you like for me to tell you about?

JOHN [*thoughtfully*]—Well, let me see.—Oh, I know, is there a story about "In the Garden"?

Mrs. Robbins—Not exactly a story, but some very interesting facts. You go over there to the table and get a songbook and find the song before I begin.

[John *gets the songbook and returns to the stool. Opens the book to the song.*]

John—O. K., Mother, I'm ready.

Mrs. Robbins—Is that your favorite song?

John—Yes, I believe it is. I always think of a beautiful flower garden when I sing it.

Mrs. Robbins—I do, too, and we have a right to. I doubt if it is the same kind of garden the writer had in mind, however. First, John, I think you will be interested to know that the writer of this hymn is C. Austin Miles.

John [*surprised*]—Why, I've heard of him! He must be a modern hymn writer.

Mrs. Robbins—Yes, he is one of the writers who lived to see how much his song meant to people. C. Austin Miles wrote both the words and music. This song is sung in many countries and in many languages. One publishing house has made more than five million impressions of it and has distributed it widely.

John—It sure is well known, isn't it?

Mrs. Robbins—Yes, it is. Well, to go on with the story now. A well-known musician by the name of Adam Geibel asked Mr. Miles to write a poem for him. He wanted a poem that would express sympathy and tenderness all the way through. He wanted one that would express hope, encouragement, rest and comfort.

John—That was a pretty big order, wasn't it?

Mrs. Robbins—It would seem that it would take a book to do all that, wouldn't it? Mr. Miles, being a very devout Christian, knew where to go to get ideas for such a poem. He went to the Bible. Did you ever have any other mental picture besides a beautiful garden when you sang this?

JOHN—Well—I always thought of some one out in the garden in the morning.

MRS. ROBBINS—No particular garden?

JOHN—No.

MRS. ROBBINS—Do you remember those passages in the Bible which say that early on the first day of the week, Mary Magdalene came to the sepulcher?

JOHN—Oh, yes, I remember.

MRS. ROBBINS—As Mr. Miles began to think about the writing of the poem he opened his Bible and read that passage. Immediately the thoughts of that first Easter came to him. You remember, Jesus was buried in a garden which belonged to Joseph of Arimathea. Mr. Miles began to picture the garden that Easter morning. He thought of the beauty of it; of how Mary came to anoint Jesus as was the custom and found that His body was gone. She went and told the disciples and they came. Failing to find Jesus, they soon went away, but Mary stayed. She stood outside the sepulcher weeping, and then Jesus came and spoke to her. You read the first stanza and see if you don't see that picture.

[JOHN *thoughtfully reads aloud the first stanza of "In the Garden."*]

JOHN—Sure enough, now that I know what Mr. Miles had in mind, I can see that it is a real garden.

MRS. ROBBINS—Now read the second stanza.

[JOHN *reads the second stanza.*]

MRS. ROBBINS—Can't you imagine that Mary Magdalene may have thought just those words? As we read the third stanza, we are reminded that it was to be Mary's duty to go and tell what had happened. She probably would rather have stayed there, but Jesus told her to go and tell others.

JOHN—That song really paints a picture, doesn't it?

MRS. ROBBINS—I think so.

JOHN—But, Mother, do you think that song has all the things in it the musician asked for?

MRS. ROBBINS—Yes, I'm sure of it. Now let's think a minute. Jesus is sympathetic; He is kind, and He brings hope to all who accept Him. Those were some of the things Mr. Geibel asked to have in the poem. Mary forgot all her sorrow and weariness and was supremely happy. It seems to me that every line tells us all these things.

JOHN—Did Mr. Miles write the music, too?

MRS. ROBBINS—Yes. Mr. Miles gave the poem to Mr. Geibel, but he didn't find a melody for it that suited him. Mr. Geibel gave it back to Mr. Miles and he wrote the music.

JOHN—I think now, instead of thinking of just a garden, I shall think of the garden of Joseph. I'll imagine Mary or some Christian walking in that garden with Jesus.

["*In the Garden*" is sung as a solo.]

CURTAIN

Have Thine Own Way

Have Thine own way, Lord,
  Have Thine own way!
Thou art the Potter;
  I am the clay.
Mold me and make me
  After Thy will,
While I am waiting,
  Yielded and still.

Have Thine own way, Lord,
  Have Thine own way!
Search me and try me,
  Master, today!
Whiter than snow, Lord,
  Wash me just now,
As in Thy presence,
  Humbly I bow.

Have Thine own way, Lord,
  Have Thine own way!
Wounded and weary,
  Help me, I pray!
Power, all power,
  Surely is Thine!
Touch me and heal me,
  Saviour divine!

Have Thine own way, Lord,
  Have Thine own way!
Hold o'er my being
  Absolute sway!
Fill with Thy Spirit
  Till all shall see
Christ only, always,
  Living in me!

—*By Adelaide Pollard.*

—Used by permission of Hope Publishing Co., copyright owner.

Have Thine Own Way

CHARACTERS

ADELAIDE POLLARD $\left\{\begin{array}{l}\text{A young woman preparing} \\ \text{for the mission field.}\end{array}\right.$

MRS. POLLARD _____Her mother

JANE BRYAN _____ A friend of Adelaide

DR. HUGHES _____Physician (dressed in white)

COSTUMES

Of about 1907.

SUGGESTIONS

The success of this hymn drama depends, in the first scene, upon the participants' showing the earnest desire Adelaide Pollard had to become a missionary. In the second scene, it depends upon a clear portrayal of the bitter disappointment she suffered and of her struggle to regain her faith.

SCENE I

[*Living-room in the* POLLARD *home.* MRS. POLLARD *is reading. A knock is heard at the door.* MRS. POLLARD *starts to rise just as* JANE BRYAN *comes in.*]

JANE—Just making myself at home as usual by coming right in. [*Sits down opposite* MRS. POLLARD.]

MRS. POLLARD—So glad you are that way, Jane. I almost think of you as my own daughter.

JANE—Now it is my turn to be glad, if you feel that way. [*Smiles.*] Where is Adelaide?

153

MRS. POLLARD—To keep track of that girl is too big a job for me. No doubt she is out shopping again.

JANE—She certainly is a busy girl—and a happy one, too.

MRS. POLLARD—Yes, she is. We are going to miss her, too, when she is gone, aren't we?

JANE—I can't even imagine how I shall get along without her. We have been just like sisters.

MRS. POLLARD—Yes, I know.

JANE—I'll venture no two girls ever had a better time at college than we did. And yet, Mrs. Pollard, we are so different in disposition.

MRS. POLLARD—Oh, I don't know that you are so different.

JANE—As different as day and night. Adelaide is always so cheerful, sees the bright side of everything and always on the alert to see the good in every one. I'm rather moody, and, if I must confess, rather critical. I guess she is just the type for a missionary. Mrs. Pollard, when we were in college, all she could talk about was when she got on the mission field. She must have thought about it all the time.

MRS. POLLARD—Jane, it has been that way ever since she was a small girl. That is one thing that makes her going easier to bear—I know it is making her happy.

JANE—I can't tell you of the dozens of times she would come in while we were at school and tell me something she had learned that would help her to teach better. I almost envy the people on the field where she will work.

MRS. POLLARD—I really think Adelaide has been fortunate to know for so long what her life's work was to be. Many young people, through no fault of their own, are forced to change their minds many times before reaching a final decision.

JANE—It is fortunate really to know what is one's life work and be able to plan for it. I have never been that fortunate. I'm doing what I am now just because it comes as near as anything to being what I enjoy. I can think of other things, however, that I could enjoy doing, too—none of them with as much sincerity and earnestness as Adelaide, though. I believe I hear her coming.

[ADELAIDE *enters, carrying several packages.*]

ADELAIDE—That sounds as if I might have been the the topic of conversation. [*Smiles.*]

JANE—You were, but nothing you would object to.

[*Lays down package and sits down, appears fatigued.*]

MRS. POLLARD—You look tired, Adelaide.

ADELAIDE—I am, and I don't feel as good as I might. I've been a little worried because I haven't heard from the mission board. With graduation activities and so much to do since coming home, I am beginning to feel I need a little more rest.

MRS. POLLARD—I wish you would slow down just a little; there is no rush. You have plenty of time to do all you have to do. Besides, you don't know that you will leave soon. There is a letter for you on the table.

[ADELAIDE *picks up letter, opens it hurriedly.*]

ADELAIDE [*happily*]—It's from the mission board. I'll soon know my fate now [*Reads letter.*] Listen to this; no more worry for me. [*Reads.*] "We are happy to inform you that the mission board has accepted your application for field mission work in India. The salary will be the same as paid all other qualified missionaries. Come as soon as possible to our office for detailed instructions. If at all possible, we hope you will be able to sail on the boat leaving in about a month. Accept our congratulations upon the appointment to this noble work. Your in His service, John L. Sanders."

[*Excitedly goes over to* MRS. POLLARD *and puts arms around her.*] Oh, Mother, I'm so happy! At last my wish has come true. It's wonderful! I can hardly believe it. Jane, I'm really going. Aren't you glad?

JANE—Of course I'm glad for you, but Adelaide, India seems so far away and such a strange land.

[ADELAIDE *returns to her chair.* MRS. POLLARD *has a far-away look as though the news has stunned her.*]

ADELAIDE—Why, Mother, has my good news made you sad? If you only knew how happy I am!

MRS. POLLARD—Not sad, dear. How could I be when it brings you such happiness? I am selfish enough, however, to dread giving you up.

ADELAIDE—Don't feel that way. I'll have so much to tell you when I return. [*Places hand on head.*] This great joy and my shopping tour together certainly have given me a headache. If you will excuse me a moment, I think I'll take a headache tablet. [*Exit.*]

MRS. POLLARD—Jane, I'm afraid Adelaide feels worse than she is willing to admit.

CURTAIN

SCENE II

[*Waiting room of a hospital.* MRS. POLLARD *is seen nervously looking through a magazine.* ADELAIDE *is in a semi-reclining position on a settee.*]

MRS. POLLARD—Tired, dear?

ADELAIDE—Yes, but what does it matter?

MRS. POLLARD—I wish you would not be so downhearted. Life has dealt you a severe blow, I know, but there is surely a brighter side.

ADELAIDE—There can't be. My life's ambition has been snatched from me. Just six months ago today I received the letter from the mission board. Five months ago, I was to have sailed for India—and now it is all over.

MRS. POLLARD—Maybe not. You are better or you wouldn't be able even to be here sitting up.

ADELAIDE [*bitterly*]—Better! What does that mean? I can't walk and I can't go to India. Sometimes I wonder if there is a God.

MRS. POLLARD—Adelaide, how can you talk like that?

ADELAIDE—And how can I be punished like this? All my life I've planned to carry the gospel to India. No, I'm through with everything. I've been cheated, that's what I have.

MRS. POLLARD—Please, don't speak that way, Adelaide.

[JANE *enters.*]

JANE—I knew you were to be brought here for a complete examination, Adelaide, and I just had to come.

MRS. POLLARD—Sit down, dear, it is so sweet of you to come. The doctors have examined Adelaide and are in consultation now.

JANE—I expected to find you in bed, Adelaide.

ADELAIDE—This is one thing in which I am having my way. I've had enough of being in bed, and I saw no reason that I couldn't remain in this private waiting room. I wanted to live for others and couldn't, and now I'm living as *I* desire.

[DR. HUGHES *appears in the door as* MRS. POLLARD *speaks. He enters and sits down.*]

MRS. POLLARD—There is Dr. Hughes now.

DR. HUGHES—Well, Mrs. Pollard, the doctors have decided that all that can be done has been done.

MRS. POLLARD [*excitedly*]—You mean—

DR. HUGHES—Now don't jump at conclusions until I have finished. I mean that unless we resort to surgery, Adelaide can never be any better than she is now.

ADELAIDE—I told you, Mother, to come here was a waste of time. Life has cheated me. I don't believe in anything. I have no confidence in anything or anybody.

DR. HUGHES—Now, Adelaide, I wouldn't be so bitter. As long as there is life there is hope.

ADELAIDE—All my hopes are shattered. I'll probably die on the table—and I don't care.

[MRS. POLLARD *covers face with handkerchief.*]

DR. HUGHES—Adelaide, you asked me when you came in to be frank with you. Your heart is in good condition, and I saw no reason that I shouldn't tell you the facts.

MRS. POLLARD—But, Dr. Hughes, what benefit can we hope to receive from surgery?

DR. HUGHES—I think you understand that our main objective is to make her walk. If the operation is successful she will walk, but she can never lead the active life she could before. The operation is a delicate one, as you know, but the best surgeon is here awaiting your decision.

ADELAIDE—I'll be an invalid any way it goes?

DR. HUGHES—Not necessarily an invalid, but you will never be able to do strenuous work. It seems to me to be able to walk is very much to be desired.

MRS. POLLARD—Indeed it is.

DR. HUGHES—However, I should like to see Adelaide in a different frame of mind if she decides upon the operation. The mental attitude has a great deal to do with our success as surgeons.

ADELAIDE—Perhaps you don't know what this means to me. My life ambition has been blasted, particularly since I had dedicated myself to serve others. But maybe there is no more merit in one ambition than another. Right or wrong, I'm bitter and indifferent.

Mrs. Pollard—How soon must we decide?

Dr. Hughes—As soon as possible. It could be done immediately if that is your desire. Dr. Major will be here several hours yet. Now I shall leave you to discuss this. Adelaide, don't be too bitter. If you only knew how I wish I could have brought you better news!

[Dr. Hughes *leaves.* Mrs. Pollard *does not speak immediately.*]

Mrs. Pollard—I only wish I knew what is the best to do.

Jane—I wish I could tell you.

Adelaide—It's immaterial to me. I have nothing to gain or lose now. I've lost all as it is.

Jane—No, not all. You are young, and if you can walk again that will be something. I'm sure there is a bright side to all this.

Mrs. Pollard—Would you rather we should leave you for a while? Maybe you can come to some decision alone.

Adelaide—I believe that would be the best.

[Mrs. Pollard *and* Jane *rise and go toward the door.*]

Mrs. Pollard—Just remember this. I am sorry this has happened, but try not to be so bitter. Try to live for my sake.

[*Exit, followed by* Jane.]

Adelaide—If I only knew what to do! Why have I been forced to give up? It isn't fair—it isn't fair. [*Remains silent for a moment.*] I must decide, and, as Jane says, maybe there is hope. I'm sorry I have been so bitter, but the disappointment has been so great. [*Bows head. Is silent a moment.*] Lord, forgive me for my bitterness. You understand, I'm sure. Help me make this decision in Thine own way. [*Raises head.*] Have Thine own way—have Thine own way. Yes, that is my decision, I'll have the operation, and if the Lord's way is followed I shall be happy. [*Begins to write on a piece of paper she has taken from her purse. Reads as she writes. Reads first two stanzas of song, "Have Thine Own Way." Choir sings these stanzas.* MRS. POLLARD *enters.* ADELAIDE *smiles.*]

ADELAIDE—Well, Mother, I've decided. I'll take the chance. All bitterness is gone. Tell Dr. Hughes I shall go at once.

[DR. HUGHES *enters.*]

MRS. POLLARD—I was just going to call you, Doctor. Adelaide has decided to have the operation at once.

ADELAIDE—Yes, I'm ready, and I shall live many happy years and useful ones. I know I shall. This explains my attitude. [*Hands* DR. HUGHES *the slip of paper with poem.*]

DR. HUGHES—Splendid! I'm sure you will [*Reads.*] If that is your attitude we need never fear. Read this, Mrs. Pollard. I shall go immediately and prepare for the operation. [*Exit.*]

MRS. POLLARD—How beautiful! That may win more souls than if you had gone to India, especially if people know how it came to be written. It is wonderful to have faith and trust enough to say you are willing for the Lord to have His own way when facing disappointments. You are a brave girl.

CURTAIN

Faith of Our Fathers

Faith of our fathers! living still
  In spite of dungeon, fire and sword;
Oh, how our hearts beat high with joy
  Whene'er we hear that glorious Word!

Refrain

Faith of our fathers, holy faith,
We will be true to thee till death.

Our fathers, chained in prisons dark,
  Were still in heart and conscience free;
How sweet would be their children's fate
    If they, like them, could die for thee!

Faith of our fathers! we will love
  Both friend and foe in all our strife;
And preach thee, too, as love knows how,
  By kindly words and virtuous life.

                          —Frederick W. Faber.

Faith of Our Fathers

CHARACTERS

READER
LUTHER _____Middle-aged
CARLSTADT _____Very fiery
MELANCHTHON _____Young student
JOHN BUNYAN _____Kindly
JAILER _____Surly
TAYLOR _____Friend of Bunyan
TED _____A young Christian
JIM _____A ne'er-do-well
BILL _____Rather easily swayed
CHOIR _____Backstage

COSTUMES

Scene I, early sixteenth century in Germany. Scene II, seventeenth century in England. Bunyan in black prison garb. Scene III, modern.

SCENE I

[*A rather bare room, containing table and chairs.*]

READER—Few Christians today realize what it has cost believers in the past to remain faithful to the truth. Here in America we can worship in perfect freedom. The struggles of the past seem remote to us. However, Frederick W. Faber has written a hymn that seeks to remind us of what it once meant to be a believer in Christianity. "Faith of Our Fathers" sings of hardships and of glorious victories.

163

It tells of the past and still reminds us to keep alive the faith that has been given to us. It seems harder, at times, to remain steadfast when there is no opposition than when persecution stares us in the face. So, let us look at a few scenes from the past and derive strength from the examples of others.

First, a picture from the life of the great reformer, Martin Luther, who began the Protestant Reformation. Luther was summoned to Worms to be tried before the Emperor, and, in our scene, his two colleagues, Dr. Carlstadt and student Melanchthon, seek to deter him.

[*The curtain rises, showing* Luther *seated at the table;* Melanchthon *stands by; while* Carlstadt *walks back and forth, agitated.*]

Carlstadt—Dr. Luther. You must not go to Worms. Your life will not be worth a groschen. They will burn you at the stake.

Luther—You are too apprehensive, Carlstadt. After all, the Emperor has promised me safe conduct.

Carlstadt—Bah, what does that mean! Huss was burned after he had been promised safety. You will not be any more fortunate.

Melanchthon—Dr. Carlstadt is right. It is a dangerous undertaking. The Emperor fears you and will take steps to see that you do not trouble him any more.

Luther—You men forget that if I do not go, all Germany will think that I am afraid. My cause will be lost, and I will be a coward in the Lord's service.

Melanchthon—You can not afford to risk your life, Dr. Luther.

Luther [*jumping up*]—I can not afford not to risk my life, Melanchthon. The cause of evangelical Christianity in Germany and throughout the world is at stake. If I falter, it will be a severe blow, for my friends and enemies look on me as the champion of my cause.

CARLSTADT—But what hope have you of returning alive?

LUTHER—I have the hope that my cause is just and right. I have the conviction that God will bring me back from Worms alive if I am to continue my work of spreading the gospel in Germany.

MELANCHTHON—You would have a chance, Dr. Luther, if the men you must face were human beings. But they are devils, plotting how they may entrap you.

LUTHER—I will go to Worms, though there be as many devils as there be tiles upon the roofs. I do not fear any force. I travel in a just cause, and the hand of God will guard me.

CARLSTADT—There seems to be no way of persuading you to relent, Dr. Luther. You are foolhardy, perhaps, but a brave man.

MELANCHTHON—Do take every precaution. If anything happens to you, our cause is lost.

LUTHER—Do not fear. I shall be careful. But the cause of true Christianity doesn't rest on any one man's shoulders, gentlemen. It is stronger than we weak mortals. I am going to Worms to testify to the faith that I have learned from the Word of God. If it be God's will, I shall return. If not, others will carry on the fight for a pure Christianity.

[*Curtain. The choir sings the first stanza of the hymn.*]

READER—And so Martin Luther went to Worms and testified to his faith. Through the intervention of powerful friends, he escaped death and carried on the Reformation. Others have not been so fortunate as Luther. John Bunyan, for example, spent twelve years in prison because he dared to preach the truth. Yet these were not idle years for the great preacher. He talked with the inmates, and, more important still, he wrote his famous book, "Pilgrim's Progress." No book except the Bible has been read by more Christians. All who have read it are touched by the simple faith of the author. Let us see a picture of the gentle Bunyan in prison.

SCENE II

[*A bleak room, with a rude table and two benches. A manuscript lies on the table.* BUNYAN *just finishes writing as the curtain goes up. A door with black adhesive tape for bars may be used at rear of room, but is not necessary.*]

JAILER [*outside door*]—Mind, you don't stay too long. Company for you, Mr. Bunyan. [*Door opens and* TAYLOR *comes in.*]

TAYLOR—Ah, dear Pastor, how are you?

BUNYAN—Taylor! I've been starved for the sight of a friendly face. Here, sit on one of my rude benches.

TAYLOR—Thank you. The jailer will allow me only a few minutes, so tell me quickly—how are you?

BUNYAN—Under God's protection, I grow and thrive, even in prison. But now, tell me something. Is the work being carried on faithfully?

TAYLOR—We are preaching the gospel to many, but we need you to give us more power.

BUNYAN—I am a reproach to my enemies as long as I remain behind these four walls. Besides, I have something else that may make hearts stronger. I have not been idle here in prison. I have been writing a book. It is all finished, and I want you to get it to a printer, Taylor.

TAYLOR—It will be almost as if you were among us again, Pastor. But are you never to be released from this cruel prison?

BUNYAN—I do not know how long God will permit my tormentors to keep me here. My faith is unshaken, however. Perhaps it was part of God's plan, so that I could write my "Pilgrim's Progress." At least, here I am, and I shall continue to put my trust in Him who does all things well.

[*Curtain. The singers sing the second stanza of the hymn.*]

READER—And so John Bunyan had his great book published. It has strengthened the faith of thousands of readers. All the persecution and suffering for religious belief is not over, however. Today we are not forced to undergo imprisonment and torture, but often the jeers of companions are just as much of a torment as threats and jail sentences. Let us see the faith of our fathers working in the youth of our modern world.

SCENE III

[*A typical room for a boy. A desk and a few chairs. Clothes scattered about.* JIM, TED *and* BILL *are talking.*]

JIM—Say, Ted, Bill and I have a keen plan for getting those radio parts we need.

TED—Boy, that's good! If we can get the rest of the parts, we can build an amateur station that will open people's eyes.

BILL—The nice part about our plan is that it won't cost us a cent to get any of the parts. How's that?

TED—Sounds too good to be true. What's the plan?

JIM—Well, you know Old Mr. Foster who has that big radio set and all of those parts?

TED—Sure. Is he going to give them to us?

BILL—Not exactly give them to us, but it amounts to the same thing.

TED—What do you mean?

BILL—He's out of town, see. Jim found that out. He also found out that the cellar window in his house is open. Now all we have to do is crawl through the window, pick up the parts we need and then we'll be all ready to broadcast.

TED—But that's stealing!

JIM—Aw, don't be a sissy. Nobody will know a thing about it. Besides, Old Man Foster's got lots of money. He'll never miss a couple of parts.

TED—I don't care. It's not right to take things when they don't belong to you.

BILL—Aw, you're just scared. That's all that's the matter with you.

TED—I'm not either. I just believe in doing what's right.

JIM—We won't have anything more to do with a coward like you. If you don't go with us, you're not our friend.

TED—My father told me never to forget that God watches all that I do. I wouldn't be able to forget that if I went with you.

JIM—Just a Sunday-school lad, that's all!

BILL—Come on, Jim, let's leave the lily alone. [*They go out and* TED *looks dejected.*]

TED [*to himself*]—Alone. [*Softly.*] "I will not leave thee nor forsake thee." [*His face grows light as the curtain falls. The choir sings the last stanza of the hymn.*]

READER—The faith of our fathers continues on from age to age. Always there are those who refuse to be swayed by threats or taunts. The roll of martyrs grows longer from year to year. But should we grow forgetful of the great deeds and victories of the past, the hymn of Frederick W. Faber will serve to stimulate our respect and to stir us on to new heights. Let us all unite in singing this great hymn [*song by the congregation*].

Silent Night, Holy Night

Silent night, holy night,
All is calm, all is bright
Round yon Virgin Mother and Child;
Holy Infant so tender and mild,
Sleep in heavenly peace,
Sleep in heavenly peace.

Silent night, holy night,
Shepherds quake at the sight,
Glories stream from heaven afar,
Heav'nly hosts sing alleluia;
Christ, the Saviour, is born,
Christ, the Saviour, is born.

Silent night, holy night,
Son of God, love's pure light
Radiant beams from Thy holy face,
With the dawn of redeeming grace;
Jesus, Lord, at Thy birth,
Jesus, Lord, at Thy birth.

—*Joseph Mohr.*

Silent Night, Holy Night

CHARACTERS

SUE RANDOLPH	A young girl
MARY RANDOLPH	Her sister
PAUL, FRANK, LOYD	Three boys
EDNA, LORA, BETTY	Three girls

(Persons taking these parts should be from the Young People's Department of the church.)

COSTUMES

The girls are in modern dress. The three boys and three girls have on their coats, indicative of the winter season.

SUGGESTIONS

The persons taking part should speak distinctly, and when telling of the writing of the hymns should not speak too hurriedly.

SCENE I

[*Living-room in the* RANDOLPH *home. A bookcase filled with books is an essential piece of furniture.* SUE *is busily straightening the room, humming as she does so.* MARY *enters, seats herself near the table and picks up a magazine.*]

MARY—Beat you this time. The dishes are finished.

SUE—I'm just about finished. It seems to me this family can scatter more magazines around than any family I know.

MARY—What's a home for if you can't use it? Personally, I think it looks more homelike if things are a little out of order.

SUE [*laughing*]—Ours will always be homelike, then.

MARY—Well, anyway, I notice all the young folks like to come here.

SUE—I know they do. They ought to be here soon, too. It's 7:30 and that's the time we set.

MARY—Time doesn't mean much at Christmastime, anyway. Every one is so busy. Do you really think it was necessary to rehearse those Christmas carols? Every one knows them.

SUE—I think it is better to. Some of us have never sung together before.

[*A noise is heard offstage. The door opens and* PAUL *enters, followed by the other young people.*]

PAUL—Anybody home? No use being so formal as to knock, says I. [*All laugh.*]

SUE—How did it ever happen that you all arrived at once? Usually we have to wait on some one.

BETTY—Christmas, Sue, Christmas, and we're all afraid of Santa Claus. [*All laugh heartily.*]

MARY—Well, you certainly are all in gay spirits, I must say. Take off your coats and find some chairs.

[MARY *and* SUE *take the coats offstage, then return. They all assume an "at home attitude."*]

FRANK—Everybody willing, what do you say we start rehearsing right away?

EDNA—You certainly are ambitious tonight. What's the idea?

FRANK—Hardly ambitious, but I have an overdue Biology paper, and my grades won't stand much cutting.

LORA—I thought so.

SUE—Well, let's get busy, then.

[*Any one of the group may take the part of the pianist. All assemble around the piano. Pianist opens the songbook, is looking through it.*]

LOYD—There is "Silent Night." Just as well start with that.

[*Two stanzas are sung.*]

BETTY—There's "O Little Town of Bethlehem" on the next page. How about that next?

[*Two stanzas are sung.*]

FRANK—Wonder where those songs ever came from?

EDNA—You know, I've wondered that a number of times.

LORA—We sing them every year, but I can't say that I ever thought about their origin.

PAUL—Who wrote them?

BETTY [*looking at song.*]—John Mohr and Franz Gruber wrote "Silent Night," whoever they are.

LOYD—I don't believe they are Americans, anyway.

BETTY—Phillips Brooks wrote "O Little Town of Bethlehem." I think I've heard of him. He wrote some of the poems we had in our readers down in the grades.

SUE—Are you sure? Men seldom write for children.

LORA—I think I remember that he did, too.

MARY—They are very old songs, I imagine.

EDNA—They probably are.

SUE—There are some books in the bookcase on the history of hymns. I've never read them, but Mother is rather interested in hymnology. It's one of her hobbies.

FRANK [*goes to bookcase and begins looking over books*]— Well, I'm interested enough to look, anyway.

[BETTY *and* PAUL *also begin looking at the books in the bookcase.* FRANK *selects one book. Sits down in a chair near the bookcase.*]

FRANK—Here is a book on hymns. Now let's see if it has "Silent Night" in it.

[BETTY *and* PAUL *each select books. All seem intensely interested.*]

BETTY—There ought to be something in here about it. It's a book on familiar hymns, and I can't think of any that is more familiar.

FRANK—Here it is. It says that both the tune and the words were written in 1818.

EDNA—It is rather old then.

LOYD—Is there anything more about it?

FRANK—Yes, there is. It was written in Obendorf, Austria, by an Austrian priest, Joseph Mohr. It seems these men had often remarked that the perfect Christmas song had never been written.

LORA—And I suppose they decided to write it.

FRANK—No, not exactly. In fact, from the account here, I don't think they ever planned on any one else's using it. Mohr sat in his study one Christmas Eve, and as he looked out of his window the stillness of the night impressed him. As he looked at the high mountain peaks he thought of the first Christmas. It was still and clear, he imagined. He wrote the words in German. The next morning he went to his friend, Franz Gruber, to show him the song. Gruber was the schoolmaster and church organist. After Gruber read it he was so enthusiastic, it is said, that he exclaimed, "God be praised! Here is the right Christmas song." So he began to compose a melody for it. The two men sang it over together. The next day they sang it before its first audience. The people were thrilled with it.

[*Several exclaim, "How interesting," etc.*]

BETTY—Now what I'd like to know is how did it ever get to be so well known?

FRANK—The book doesn't say anything about that.

PAUL—I can answer that, and it's interesting, too. This book on hymnology says that for nearly a year after the two men sang it, the song was practically forgotten. The next year the organ had to be repaired. The organ mechanic asked Gruber to test the organ. Gruber remembered the melody to "Silent Night" and used it to test the organ. The man who was repairing the organ thought it so beautiful he asked for a copy. Gruber gave it to him, and the man took it to his home in the mountains.

EDNA—That still doesn't tell us how it came to America.

PAUL—Give me time and I'll tell you more. Well, in this village where the organ repair man lived, the four Strasser sisters lived. These girls were trained singers, and they later sang this song in the large Cathedral of Leipzig, in Germany. From this rendition it passed from one music lover to another. Here is an interesting fact, however—it was called, "The Tyrolese Song" for twenty-four years after Gruber wrote it, because these men lived in the Tyrole Mountains.

SUE—That is interesting; it makes the song mean more when I know its history. No wonder Mother says hymnology is interesting.

LORA—While we're looking up about hymns I'd like to know more about "O Little Town of Bethlehem."

FRANK—I looked it up in this book but it isn't given.

BETTY—It is in here.

LORA—Good. What about it?

BETTY—It was written in 1868, by Phillips Brooks. He was rector of the Holy Trinity Church, in Philadelphia. The church gave him a year's vacation and he went to the Holy Land, in the year 1865. On Christmas Eve, he and his friends went from Jerusalem to Bethlehem. At one place they could look across at the town of Bethlehem. It seemed so still and dark compared with American towns. He saw the shepherds still tending their sheep. Brooks and his friends attempted to locate the field where the shepherds saw the star. He was so impressed . . .

LORA—That he wrote the song.

BETTY—Oh, no, not yet. Time after time, upon his return, he would meditate on this scene. In the year 1868, he decided to write a song for the Sunday school's Christmas program. He tried in verse to picture the town of Bethlehem. Then he took the poem to the church organist, Lewis Redner, and he wrote the tune for it. The next Sunday being Christmas, the children of Brooks' Sunday school sang "O Little Town of Bethlehem" for the first time.

PAUL—This book says that Redner had a little difficulty finding a melody he liked. He awoke one night, and it seemed he could hear the melody being sung. He got up and wrote it. And here's another thing I'll venture none of us knew. There was originally a fourth stanza.

LOYD—Well, what do you know about that? I've never seen it in a hymnbook.

PAUL—No, none of us has. Phillips Brooks himself omitted it because of some criticism.

MARY—I don't know how the rest of you feel, but I'm glad our curiosity led us to investigate all this.

SUE—Are we going to rehearse any more tonight?

BETTY—It's getting too late, don't you think?

LOYD—Let's sing one stanza of "Silent Night" and then go home. Personally, I think we have accomplished more than if we had practiced all evening.

[*They sing one stanza of "Silent Night."*]

CURTAIN

176

Come, Thou Fount of Every Blessing!

Come, Thou Fount of every blessing,
   Tune my heart to sing Thy grace;
Streams of mercy, never ceasing,
   Call for songs of loudest praise.

Teach me some celestial measure,
   Sung by ransomed hosts above;
Oh, the vast, the boundless treasure
   Of my Lord's unchanging love!

Oh, to grace how great a debtor,
   Daily I'm constrained to be!
Let Thy grace, Lord, like a fetter,
   Bind my wand'ring heart to Thee.

Prone to wander, Lord, I feel it—
   Prone to leave the God I love—
Take my heart, oh, take and seal it,
   Seal it from Thy courts above.

                  —Robert Robinson.

Come, Thou Fount of Every Blessing!

CHARACTERS

ROBERT ROBINSON _____ _____The writer of the song
JIM BRYANT, HENRY WILSON _____His chums
MRS. LANE _____ A member of Mr. Robinson's church

COSTUMES

The first scene takes place in the year 1752, and the second in 1757. Costumes should be of this period, or clothing and furnishings similar to those of the nineteenth century may be used.

COMMENTS

At the time of the first scene, Robert has fallen into rather evil company. The second scene is after his conversion and he is a minister. Jim Bryant, Henry Wilson and Mrs. Lane are fictitious characters. The main happenings are true.

SCENE I

[ROBERT'S *room in a boarding-house.* JIM *and* HENRY *are in* ROBERT'S *room, waiting for* ROBERT *to return. The boys are rather untidy in appearance.*]

JIM—Wonder where Bob is?

HENRY—I don't know; he has surely finished work by now.

JIM—Can't tell. That hairdresser keeps him all hours. Had a late customer maybe.

HENRY—I wouldn't like that work, would you?

JIM—No. [*Hesitates.*] One job is as good as another if you get your money, though, I guess.

HENRY—As long as I can eat, that's all I care.

JIM—No work, no eat—that's my trouble.

HENRY—Bob acts rather queer lately, don't you think?

JIM—Rather.

HENRY—Wonder what's wrong with him.

JIM—I don't know; but there's something.

HENRY—He's never been the same since we took the liquor to that fortune-teller. You remember that Sunday night a while back?

JIM—Why blame her? She's a fraud anyway.

HENRY—I know, but Bob acts different since we were there.

JIM—Maybe he believes in them. Do you?

HENRY—Sometimes yes, and sometimes no.

JIM—I'd say all the time no. How could they know what's in the future?

HENRY—I don't know. She didn't tell him anything to be worried about, do you think?

JIM—He's a good fellow, but queer. Has he any people?

HENRY—I guess his mother is still alive. His father's been dead several years. That's the reason he came to London. He said that his mother couldn't keep him.

JIM—I'm doing all right without parents. How about you?

HENRY—I guess so. Here he comes.

[ROBERT *enters; appears fatigued. Tosses cap on the floor and slumps in a chair. The conversation starts as he enters.*]

Jim—Hello, Bob.

Henry—Making ourselves at home. Had begun to think you were lost.

Robert—Glad to see you fellows. Waited long?

Henry—Not very. Tired?

Robert—Yes, in more ways than one.

Jim—Big day?

[Robert *seems in deep thought.* Henry *waits and then speaks. Looks at* Robert *in questioning manner.*]

Henry—Don't like our company?

[Henry *and* Jim *laugh.*]

Robert [*startled*]—Huh? Some one say something to me?

Jim—What's the matter? Bad news?

Robert—Nothing's the matter. I guess I was just thinking.

Jim—Henry said that you had been acting strangely. We're your friends; tell us.

Henry—Sure. Tell us; if we can help we will. Always have, haven't we?

Robert—It's nothing, boys. [*Walks across the floor, then returns to his chair.*] At least nothing you can help me with.

Jim—Well, tell us anyway.

Henry—You surely aren't brooding over some of the nonsense that fortune-teller told you, are you?

Robert [*hesitatingly*]—She at least started me thinking.

Jim—Now, why even think about anything she told you? Just because we took some liquor to her house, and, in order to have a little fun, let her tell our fortunes, you act like you have lost your last friend.

Henry—I agree, it's silly. You never acted like this over anything before.

ROBERT—Fortune-teller or no fortune-teller, there's something we ought to think about.

HENRY—Now what?

ROBERT—I'll admit that fortune-teller did say one thing that made me think. Now understand this: First, I don't believe in any of her prophecies. She doesn't know any more about the future than I do. She may guess at it and hit it sometimes. Here is what I started out to tell you. She said that I would see my children and even my grandchildren.

HENRY—Well, what of it?

JIM—I probably will, too, but who cares?

ROBERT—I've been thinking that we have a responsibility if that is the case.

JIM—I don't understand you.

ROBERT—Do you think you would want your children to lead the life we are? Would you be proud or ashamed if they knew the kind of life we lived as young men?

HENRY—It's none of their business. If we don't have a good time now, when can we expect to?

ROBERT—That's just it. Are we having a good time? I'm not. Oh, I think at the time I am, but afterwards it worries me. We do a lot of things that are not right; you both know it and so do I.

HENRY [*laughing*]—The next thing we know he will be telling us he is going to church. [HENRY *and* JIM *both laugh.* ROBERT *remains very quiet.*]

ROBERT [*determined*]—All right, boys, I have gone to church, and I'm not ashamed of it.

JIM [*excited and astonished*]—You have what! Been to church?

ROBERT—Yes, been to church. That's where I was tonight. A preacher by the name of George Whitfield is holding services here. I heard him speak on the subject of future wrath in the judgment. I'm convinced we are to face a judgment, and I certainly don't care to with the life I'm living now.

JIM—Scared, are you?

ROBERT—No, I'm not scared. If Jesus thought enough of us to die for us, I ought to think enough of myself to live respectably. You may as well know the rest—I'm going to become a minister.

HENRY [*amazed*]—I can't believe it. I don't know what to say. I can't make fun of you, for maybe you are right.

JIM—Will wonders never cease?

ROBERT—I know I'm right. I wish you boys would do the same.

HENRY—Don't think that's the life for me. Let's go, Jim. [HENRY *and* JIM *start toward door.*]

ROBERT—Don't go; I'd like to talk to you.

JIM—No, I'm afraid we haven't much in common.

[*Both boys leave.* ROBERT *is silent, then speaks.*]

ROBERT—Looks like my friends, or what I thought were friends, will forsake me. I can give them up, for this peace and satisfaction is worth more. If I'm to lead the Christian life, I'll have to expect such things. It's worth it. I hope I never lose this joy that has come to me.

CURTAIN

SCENE II

[MR. ROBINSON'S *study in the church where he is minister. He is talking with* MRS. LANE.]

MRS. LANE—Brother Robinson, I have been so worried about my boy. He takes no interest in church nor any of the better things of life. I'm afraid the company he keeps is having a bad influence on him. What can I do?

MR. ROBINSON—I realize and understand your problem thoroughly. It's a difficult situation. Have you talked to him? That may sound absurd to ask, but some parents do hesitate.

MRS. LANE—Yes, so many times. He thinks I am just a back number.

MR. ROBINSON [*smiling*]—Quite naturally. Then I would suggest if you know some one in whom he has a great deal of confidence that you ask him to talk with him.

MRS. LANE—I can't think of any one he has confidence in to any great extent.

MR. ROBINSON—I have found it difficult to get acquainted with him. However, if I can be of any help, I should be very happy to talk to him. He may change very suddenly, you can never tell. It may be only a very simple statement that starts him to thinking. It may not even be a remark by a Christian. These minds of ours respond very strangely to suggestion. Then we must always resort to prayer. Keep up your faith. I'm sure it will turn out all right. Your son is no doubt sowing a little wild oats. They may prove to be dangerous, of course, but let him know you have faith in him.

MRS. LANE—You are so kind and understanding. It is a little hard for me to understand how one who has never faced temptation can be so understanding.

MR. ROBINSON [*smiling*]—Mrs. Lane, I seldom mention this, but since it may be of help to you, I'm going to tell you. I was once a worse boy than yours.

MRS. LANE—I can't believe it.

MR. ROBINSON—I'm sorry to have to admit it, but it is true. I was young when my father died. My mother had no money, so I went to work in London. I began to associate with companions of a questionable nature. One night we took some liquor to a fortune-teller. Just for amusement we permitted her to tell our fortunes. She made a statement that I would have children and grandchildren. It got me to thinking of my responsibility in the future. Now don't misunderstand me; I do not endorse fortune-tellers. I couldn't get it off my mind. Later, I went to church, and it was there I really started to think. The minister preached a wonderful sermon, and I became a Christian and decided to become a minister. I can never in words tell you how happy I was because of my decision. So you see I understand what your boy may be going through. My prayers are that he will be guided aright. [*Smiles.*] Just before you came in I was reminiscing. I am still so thankful for the peace I've found as a Christian; and while the temptations have come, I've managed to remain steadfast. While I was thinking about my conversion today, I wrote a little poem about it. Would you like to see it?

MRS. LANE—Indeed I would.

[*Hands* MRS. LANE *a sheet of paper. Singers offstage sing the song.*]

MRS. LANE—How very beautiful! It may guide others as it has guided you.

CURTAIN

* Library of
Drexel Pursifull
Please Return